HOME REPAIR AND IMPROVEMENT

THE OLD HOUSE

BY THE EDITORS OF TIME-LIFE BOOKS, ALEXANDRIA, VIRGINIA

The Consultants

Louis V. Genuario Sr. received an M.S. degree in civil engineering from Harvard University before he became a career officer in the U.S. Army Corps of Engineers. He is chairman of the board of Genuario Construction Company, Inc., in northern Virginia and past president of the Alexandria chapter of the Northern Virginia Building Industry Association.

Jeff Palumbo is a registered journeyman carpenter who has a home-building and remodeling business in northern Virginia. His interest in carpentry was sparked by his grandfather, a master carpenter with more than 50 years' experience. Mr. Palumbo teaches in the Fairfax County Adult Education Program.

Mark M. Steele is a professional home inspector in the Washington, D.C., area. He has developed and conducted training programs in home-ownership skills for first-time homeowners. He appears frequently on television and radio as an expert in home repair and consumer topics.

CONTENTS

1 LOOKING BEFORE YOU BUY   6

How Old Houses Are Framed   8

Inspecting the Outside of a House   10

Checking the Top and the Bottom   15

Examining the Living Spaces   18

Assessing the Wiring   20

Looking at Old Plumbing   22

Evaluating a Heating System   24

Finding the Right Specialist   26

2 PRESERVING OLD GLORIES   28

Restoring Fine Details   30

New Life for Marble and Leaded Glass   34

Reviving Old Wood Trim   40

Remedies for Failing Plaster   46

Handsome Old Floors   52

Repairs for Balky Windows and Doors   58

3 MAKING DO WITH OLD UTILITIES   66

Safe and Efficient Fireplaces   68

Reviving Old Wiring   73

Living with a Vintage Heating System   77

Coping with Antique Plumbing   82

4 MAINTAINING A SOUND STRUCTURE   88

Keeping a Roof in Good Condition   90

Bandaging Surface Cracks   97

Shields against Moisture and Dirt   100

Patching Holes in Stucco   104

Restoring Outside Walls   106

Correcting Floor Sags   112

Remedies for Ailing Foundations   122

Index   126

Acknowledgments   128

Picture Credits   128

Looking Before You Buy

A stately old house is a beautiful sight, but living in one can raise concerns about safety, convenience, and economy. To appreciate what may confront you, begin looking for serious flaws on your first visit, according to the methods in this chapter. Once you move in, it's wise to complete repairs to the house structure and services (wiring, heating, and plumbing) before you turn to painting and other cosmetic improvements.

How Old Houses Are Framed   8

Inspecting the Outside of a House   10

Starting at the Roof
Evaluating the Walls

Checking the Top and the Bottom   15

A Look at the Basement
Surveying the Attic

Examining the Living Spaces   18

Assessing the Wiring   20

Looking at Old Plumbing   22

Evaluating a Heating System   24

Finding the Right Specialist   26

How Old Houses Are Framed

When evaluating an old house—both for existing problems and for possible improvements—you need an understanding of its basic structure. The framework, which is hidden behind finished surfaces, may seem mysterious and complex; in fact, construction methods have under-gone only a few fundamental changes since colonial times.

Early American Structures: The first wood-frame houses—as distinct from log houses—were built in the northern colonies in the 1630s. Using designs developed in the Middle Ages, colonial carpenters notched and pegged together massive posts and beams to assemble a formidable boxlike frame atop a fieldstone or brick foundation. Heavy diagonal braces at each corner gave the structures their name—braced-frame houses. Unlike most of the timbers, the floor joists were small; a huge beam (called a "summer" beam, from the French *somme,* for "burden") was there-fore centered in any span exceeding 20 feet. Sheath-ing—typically of wide boards 1 inch thick—covered the studs, and lapped clapboards or shingles were nailed to the sheathing.

Balloon and Platform Framing: Construction of wood houses was revolutionized in 1833 by the inven-tion of the balloon frame—a name conferred by critics, who compared its stud walls to the skin of a balloon. The balloon frame placed small timbers such as 2-by-4 studs close together so that they could bear the same weight as the heavier, widely spaced posts and beams of a braced-frame house. Much easier to erect, this type of frame soon became the building method of choice.

In the balloon frame, long 2-by-4s rose all the way from the foundation sill plate to the second- or third-floor rafters. The early 20th century saw the emergence of a variant—called the western, or platform, frame—with short studs topped by an intermediate plate at each story. These shorter studs are virtually identical with those used in modern homes.

Old-Style Brick: Brick houses were built as early as the mid-1600s, but they did not become widespread until the second half of the 19th century, when efficient mass production of bricks was developed. The basic design, which combined bearing walls of brick or stone with interior wood framing set into pockets in the ma-sonry, remained essentially unchanged well into the 20th century.

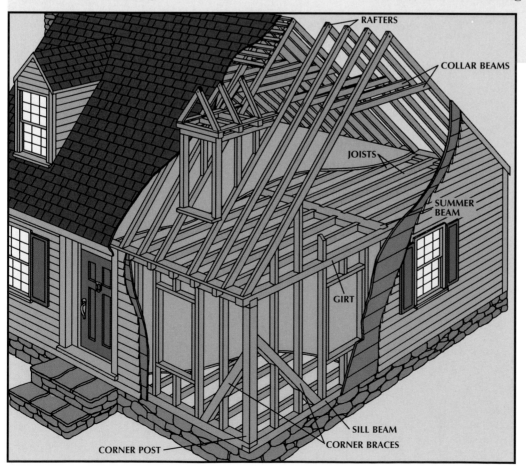

RAFTERS

COLLAR BEAMS

JOISTS

SUMMER BEAM

GIRT

SILL BEAM

CORNER BRACES

CORNER POST

The colonial braced-frame house.
In this 18th-century house, four massive sill beams, lap jointed at the corners, rest on a stone foundation wall. Strong vertical posts at the corners and along front and rear walls support four hori-zontal beams, called girts, which serve as second-story plates. A huge summer beam—running the length of the house and notched into the girts at each end—gives extra support for second-floor joists; diagonal braces rein-force each corner. The rafters meet at the peak in pegged mortise and tenon joints and are braced by collar beams.

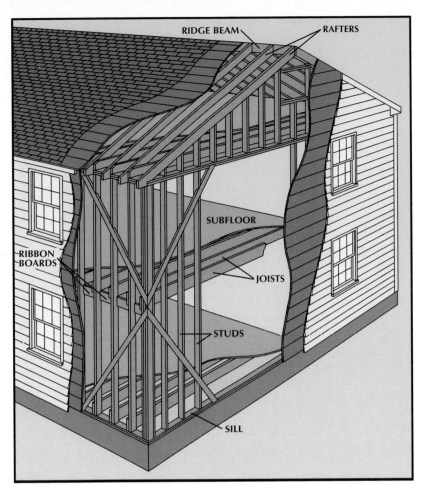

The balloon frame.

This balloon-frame house relies for its support on small timbers nailed in place. The 2-by-4 wall studs, on 16-inch centers, rise unbroken from the sills to the rafters; at the corners, 2-by-4s are nailed together to form posts. The 2-by-8 floor joists nailed to the studs are supported by sills at the first-floor level and by ribbon boards—1-by-4s notched into the studs—at higher floors. The rafters are nailed to a ridge beam at the peak.

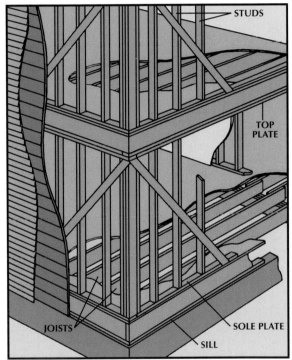

The platform frame.

In platform framing *(right),* the joists and subfloor are laid first, forming the platform for the ground-floor walls. These consist of 2-by-4 studs the height of only one story, rising from a single 2-by-4 sole plate to a doubled 2-by-4 top plate. The joists, sub-floor, and stud walls of the second floor are stacked onto the framing of the first floor in the same way.

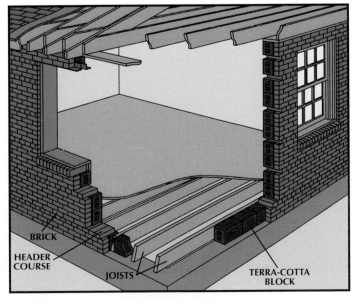

A solid-masonry house.

The walls of this early-20th-century masonry bungalow consist of a single thickness, or wythe, of hollow terra-cotta block covered by a layer of brick. (In older houses, the in-ner layer is usually brick instead of terra-cotta block; in newer ones, it is cinder block or concrete block.) The brick is mortared to the blocks, and at regular intervals—in this case, every seventh course—a header course of bricks is laid down perpendicular to the wall between block courses to further secure the bricks to the blocks. Floor joists are set on top of the foundation wall between blocks. In many houses, the first-floor joists are supported in the center of their span by a girder over a masonry pier.

Some modern houses that appear to be brick are actually wood-frame structures. A layer of nonstructural brick ve-neer is secured to the sheathing and studs with metal ties, giving the house a masonry exterior.

Begin with the exterior in any examination of a house you are seriously considering buying. A thorough inspection of the kind described on the following pages takes at least 2 hours and requires binoculars, a magnet, and an awl.

Checking for Water Damage: Your examination of the roof, gutters, and downspouts *(page 11)* will include areas vulnerable to leaks. Gutter runs longer than 40 feet should have two downspouts. If gutters and downspouts have deteriorated, masonry, wood-siding, and stucco walls may show signs of rot or crumbling *(pages 13-14)*.

Insect Damage: Before checking for infestation, past or present *(page 14)*, ask local exterminators about the most common insects in the area. An exterminator must be hired to eliminate termites, carpenter ants, and powderpost beetles—which can cause serious structural damage.

Surface Drainage: Make sure that the soil next to the foundation has been graded so it noticeably slopes away from the house for at least 6 feet. If the ground is level or slopes toward the foundation, look for signs of a wet basement and foundation damage *(page 15)*. Improper grading can be corrected by filling around the foundation with earth.

Check walkways and driveways for cracks and sinking. Generally, pavement that has sunk more than 1 inch is hazardous and is best replaced. Low points in a driveway should have a functioning drain, particularly if the driveway slopes toward the house.

Retaining walls need weep holes near the bottom for drainage. A wall that leans forward more than 1 inch for each foot of its height may have to be rebuilt.

In the Garage: Make certain that garage doors work smoothly and that a garage-door opener reverses direction when it encounters resistance. Look for a 4-inch step descending from the house to an attached garage to prevent gasoline fumes, which are heavier than air, from entering the house.

CAUTION

Safety Procedures for Lead Paint and Asbestos

Lead and asbestos, known health hazards, pervade houses constructed or remodeled before 1978. Whereas lead is found primarily in paint, potential asbestos locations include wallboard, joint compound, insulation, flooring and related adhesives, roofing felt, shingles, and flashing. A visual inspection cannot determine the presence of lead or asbestos, but you may ask that the seller get testing done. Depending on the terms of the sale, you may be responsible for removal, which can be costly. Hire a professional licensed in hazardous-substance removal for large jobs indoors or if you suffer from cardiac, respiratory, or heat-tolerance problems that may be triggered by the protective clothing and respirator you must wear to do the work yourself. Tackle a roof only if you are experienced working at heights, and remember that the respirator impairs

vision. If you remove asbestos or lead yourself, follow these procedures:

❗*Keep children, pregnant women, and pets away from the area.*

❗*Indoors, seal off work area openings with 6-mil polyethylene sheeting and duct tape. Cover rugs and non-movable furniture with more sheeting and tape. Turn off air conditioning and forced-air heating systems.*

❗*When you finish indoor work, mop the area twice, then run a vacuum cleaner equipped with a high efficiency particulate air (HEPA) filter.*

❗*Cover the work area ground outside with 6-mil polyethylene sheeting. Never work in windy conditions.*

❗*If you must use an electric sander on lead paint, get one equipped with a*

HEPA filter. Never sand asbestos-laden materials or cut them with power machinery. Instead, mist them with water and detergent, and remove them carefully with hand tools.

❗*On a roof, pry up shingles, misting as you go. Place all debris in a polyethylene bag; never throw roofing material containing asbestos to the ground.*

❗*Always wear protective clothing (available from a safety equipment supply house or paint stores) and a dual-cartridge respirator. Remove the clothing, including shoes, before leaving the work area. Wash the clothing separately, and shower and wash your hair immediately.*

❗*Dispose of the materials as recommended by your local health department or environmental protection office.*

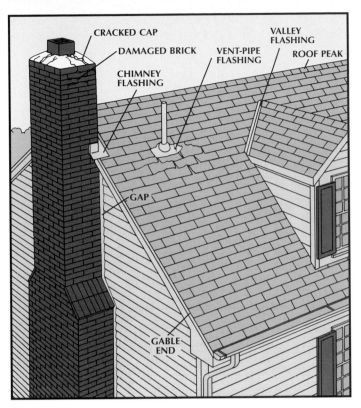

Critical areas on the roof.

◆ Using binoculars, compare the appearance of the roof with the photographs overleaf. Look at the edge of the roof along the gable. If you can see more than one generation of shingles, they must all be removed prior to reroofing.

◆ Check for sags along the ridge.

◆ Inspect exposed flashing around the chimney, in roof valleys, and around any protruding pipes. Bent, rusted, or cracked flashing requires immediate attention; look for corresponding water damage inside.

◆ Inspect the joint between the side of the house and the chimney. A gap narrower than 3 inches at the top is caused by gradual settling and should be watched for any enlargement. A wider gap may mean that the footing under the chimney is failing; consult a foundation engineer.

◆ In both exterior and interior chimneys, look for loose or damaged bricks and gaps in mortar joints and for a cracked, chipped chimney cap. Such flaws admit water, which can further damage the masonry and constitute a fire hazard, since sparks may escape into wood framing. Remedy these defects before using the fireplace.

Faulty gutters and downspouts.

◆ Examine steel or copper gutters—a magnet sticks to steel—for signs of corrosion, especially at joints and along the bottoms, where leaves might collect.

◆ Check downspouts made of any material for a separated seam along the back, often caused by clogging and freezing.

◆ Step away from the house to confirm that no gutter has pulled away from the fascia and that each slopes along the fascia board toward its downspout.

◆ Look for splash blocks or drainpipes at the ends of downspouts. Make sure splash blocks are in good condition and positioned to direct water away from the foundation. Confirm that drainpipes are not clogged.

Wherever you spot a fault in a gutter system, examine the nearby soffit and fascia board, the siding below, and the wood framing at ground level. Look for peeling paint, dark rot spots, or other signs of water damage.

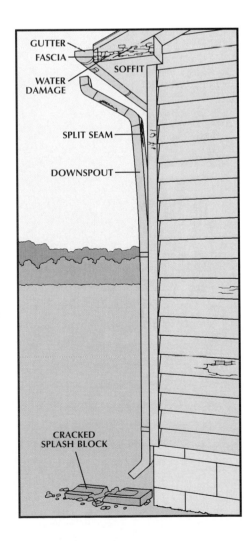

ESTIMATING THE LIFE OF A ROOF

As illustrated by the pairs of photographs below—the left-hand picture shows a new roof, and the right-hand one shows an aging roof of the same material—you can tell a lot about the condition of a roof and its life expectancy just by looking at it.

When evaluating a roof, look most closely at the southern exposure of the house, if it has one. Also, distinguish between localized damage that can be repaired and widespread deterioration that only a new roof can correct.

Repairable problems include a few broken shingles, isolated shingle leaks, or leaks around flashing *(pages 90-92)*.

However, if more than 25 percent of the shingles are broken or the roof looks substantially worse than the right-hand examples below, the house will need a new roof soon—as it will if you detect leaks in the flashing at valleys (where the roof of one part of the house meets the roof of another).

Asphalt shingles. The curling evident here signifies this roof is near the end of its 20- to 25-year life span. Rust stains *(above, right)* from old flashing are harmless to the shingles, but the flashing should be replaced.

Cedar shakes. Weathering soon turns cedar gray, so color is no indicator of age. But this roof, with almost every shake split and curling, is near the end of its 35-year life span. Cedar shingles, thinner than shakes, last 25 years at most.

Slate. More expensive than any other material, slate makes a roof that can last as long as a century. When slate surfaces flake, as these do, or show white stains, the roof is within about 10 years of requiring replacement.

Metal. With application of rustproofing, a metal roof may last 50 years or more. Though bare in spots and beginning to rust, this old roof has no broken seams. It can be saved by painting preceded by thorough preparation.

Scrutinizing wood siding.

From each corner of the house, look down the horizontal lines of the siding for any dip in the boards at the far corner. A noticeable dip indicates a sinking corner, often caused by rot or insect damage in the wood framing inside the wall or by a sinking foundation. This constitutes a serious structural problem and requires consultation with a structural engineer.

◆ Examine the siding boards for curling and cracking, and with an awl probe any rotted-looking areas *(left)*. If the awl penetrates easily more than $\frac{1}{2}$ inch, the rot needs repair. Slightly bowed boards can be nailed back in place and small areas of rot patched with fiberglass *(pages 97-98)*. But extensive rot or cracks all the way through the board along more than half its length call for new boards.
◆ Check the paint on the walls: The more layers, the harder it will be to achieve a smooth finish with new paint.

Spotting a faulty brick wall.

Examine the wall for bulging in the brick, especially near the bottom of the wall and midway up the wall near windows. Bulges indicate mortar failure in solid-masonry construction or deteriorated ties between brick veneer and the frame of a house. Although these bulges generally affect only the area where they occur and rarely threaten the entire house, they may require major work in a few years.

◆ Probe mortar joints with an awl *(right)*. If the mortar seems to be soft or sandy and falls out of the joints easily you must undertake the time-consuming job of repointing—scraping and refilling the joints *(page 123)*.
◆ Examine the mortar for gaps longer than 1 inch. A few spaces can be refilled, but many may require a mason to determine whether foundation settling may be threatening the entire house.

Evaluating bulges in stucco walls.

◆ To spot bulges, examine stucco walls at an oblique angle.

◆ By applying light pressure *(left)*, check for resilience of small bulges—generally caused by localized separation between the stucco and underlying lath—and listen for a hollow sound when you tap them.

◆ If an entire wall bulges at the center, the house may have a major structural flaw—either undersized framing members that will require strengthening *(pages 112-121)* or uneven settlement of the foundation *(pages 122-125)*.

◆ All bulges and major cracks in stucco should be repaired as soon as possible, to prevent water damage inside the wall.

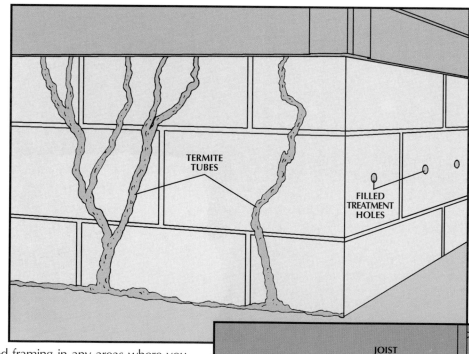

Detecting insect damage.

◆ Along foundation walls and wherever wood members are near the ground—as in a crawlspace with a dirt floor—look for termite tubes (mud tunnels built by these wood eaters) and small piles of fine sawdust signifying boring.

◆ With an awl, probe the wood framing in any areas where you suspect present or past infestation. The presence of termite shields—metal barriers installed between the foundation and framing *(inset)*—should not deter you from your inspection, since such shields are often ineffective.

◆ Note evidence of previous termite treatment: $\frac{3}{4}$-inch-diameter holes refilled with mortar in masonry walls or in the concrete floor of a basement. Prior treatment is not necessarily a bad sign, for it may have been done to forestall termites.

Thorough inspections of the lowest and topmost levels of a potential purchase are as important as evaluations of the exterior and the living spaces. All you need to examine both basement and attic are a flashlight, some string, an awl, a ruler—and the modest tool shown on page 17.

Assessing the Underpinnings: In an unfinished basement, the structural soundness of the house can be checked, since both the foundation and the framing members are visible *(overleaf)*. If drainage around a house is poor, large and small foundation cracks alike *(page 16)* may allow ground water to seep in. A wet or excessively damp basement—or one that shows signs of flooding—

may require modifications such as regrading the earth near the house, repairing gutters, or installing a sump pump *(pages 122-123)*.

Water Damage in the Attic: The attic reveals important elements such as the underside of the roof and its framing, vent pipes, and insulation *(page 17)*. When checking for roof leaks in the attic, remember that water flows unpredictably down framing members. Correlate any water paths you detect in the attic with your survey of the interior *(pages 18-19)*.

Controlling Air Flow: Proper ventilation and insulation are essential in an attic. Without both, condensation

that forms in winter when warm house air meets cool attic air may cause moisture damage to framing, insulation, and wiring. In summer, hot air from an unvented attic will radiate down into the house. Check that existing vents—along the ridge or at the gable ends—are unobstructed. If there are no vents, look for moisture damage.

Conversion and Fire Protection: Throughout the attic inspection, note available storage space and the feasibility of a later conversion to living space. In a row house, where masonry walls between houses are shared, the brick or block should rise to the roof to serve as a fire wall between your attic and those adjacent to it.

 SAFETY TIPS

When working in attics with low overhead space, a hard hat protects your head from sharp protruding nails.

A LOOK AT THE BASEMENT

Detecting signs of flooding.
◆ Examine basement floors and walls for water stains with a flashlight. Check for rust stains and mud on the floor at the base of the furnace—telltale evidence of flooding otherwise disguised by repainting *(right)*.
◆ Throughout the basement, inspect the walls for efflorescence (rough white deposits caused by

water reacting with the minerals in mortar); look at any low-lying woodwork, such as baseboards, for dark spots of rot; and check tile floors for white, powdery deposits—efflorescence from the underlying concrete.
◆ Note how things are stored: Unused furniture and storage boxes kept on raised platforms sometimes imply flooding.

Analyzing cracks.
Horizontal cracks in a bulging wall or vertical cracks in a corner of the basement that widen to $\frac{1}{4}$ inch or more at the top of the wall are cause for concern *(right)*. They are attributable either to water damage—which necessitates the correction of grading outside the wall *(page 122)*—or to foundation failure unrelated to flooding. Either of these types of cracking—which may be camouflaged with different shades of mortar from repeated patching—can threaten the integrity of an entire wall; consult a foundation engineer for a precise diagnosis. Smaller cracks—common in old houses—pose no threat to the structure but may be a source of leaks.

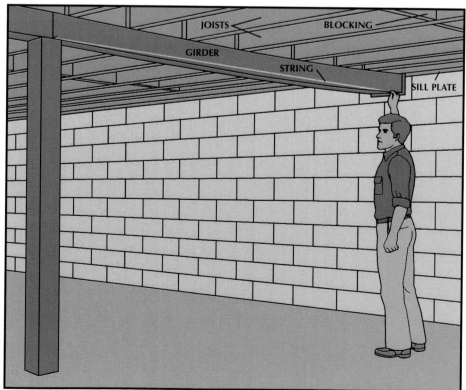

Examining wood framing.
◆ To check for sag in a girder or joist, tack a string taut between opposite bottom corners of the board *(left)*; if it droops below the string more than 1 inch in 12 feet, it needs additional support.
◆ Scrutinize all exposed framing members—joists, girders, sill plates, and the subfloor above (if any)—for rot or insect damage *(pages 13-14)*.
◆ Check for solid blocking or X-shaped bracing between joists, an indication of sturdy construction.

16

SURVEYING THE ATTIC

Inspecting the roof framing.
◆ Examine all structural members for signs of rot, insects, or water damage, probing suspect areas with an awl *(right)*. If more than four consecutive rafters are rotted, rebuilding of the roof may be in order; consult a professional.
◆ Check that vent pipes—for plumbing or a kitchen fan—discharge outside.
◆ Look for rust streaks from nailheads, and for other water stains, on the roof sheathing and around chimneys and vent pipes.

Evaluating attic insulation.
◆ In an unfinished attic, insert a ruler alongside several joists to measure the thickness of any insulation present *(left)*. For energy efficiency, temperate climates require at least a 6-inch thickness of insulation.
◆ If there is new blanket or batt insulation laid between joists, make sure the vapor barri-er—a shiny foil—faces down, toward the warmth of the house. New insulation laid atop old should have no vapor barrier, which would trap moisture in the lower layer.

To check the insulation in an attic with a floor, look for knotholes or missing floorboards near the bottoms of rafters.

In Search of Insulation

Poor attic insulation signals that wall insulation may also be inadequate. To check insulation within a wall, use the homemade tool shown here. To make one, cut, with long-nose pliers, an 8-inch length of wire from a coat hanger, then bend one end to form a $\frac{1}{2}$-inch hook. Before proceeding, turn off power to a room at the service panel, then remove an electrical outlet cover. Insert the hook between the outlet box and the wall, and snag a bit of insulation for examination. If you find loose-fill insulation, repeat the procedure at a light switch to help gauge how much the insulation has settled.

TRICKS OF THE TRADE

Examining the Living Spaces

Although a dispassionate examination of living spaces is not always easy, the walls, floors, windows, fireplaces, and other elements of the finished interior all require close scrutiny. In addition to revealing possible problems, a careful walk-through will help you estimate the potential expenses of painting and other redecoration.

Anticipating Repairs: Sometimes visible damage in the finished interior will correlate with flaws noted earlier—a water-stained ceiling beneath a suspected leak in the at-

tic, for example. By the same token, if the attic and basement were reassuring, the problems with the interior are likely to be minor and the fixes straightforward. For instance, damaged and squeaky floorboards can be readily restored *(pages 52-57)*, and even substantially damaged plaster on ceilings and walls can be replaced inexpensively with wallboard *(pages 46-48)*.

Since empty rooms have a way of looking larger than furnished ones, take time to measure rooms to make sure they will hold your possessions comfortably.

SAFETY TIPS *When inspecting fireplaces, wear safety goggles to keep falling debris out of your eyes, a dust mask to prevent the inhalation of soot and dust, and work gloves to avoid abrasions from rough edges or cracked mortar.*

Cracked walls and ceilings.

◆ Inspect plaster walls and ceilings for areas of heavy patching and any cracks wider than $\frac{1}{4}$ inch. Wide vertical cracks in a corner, horizontal cracks widening toward the center along the intersection of the ceiling and a partition wall, or large cracks that radiate from doorframes and window frames generally indicate weak or twisted wall framing.
◆ If a crack wider than $\frac{3}{8}$ inch crosses the center of a ceiling, look for a visible sag, indicating that the plaster is pulling away from its lath—a condition that requires immediate re-

plastering or patching with gypsum wallboard.
◆ Check for gaps between walls and the floor or ceiling; they are signs of serious structural problems.
◆ Check doors to see that they operate smoothly and fit precisely in their jambs, and note the quality of the hardware. Door tops planed at angles or wedge-shaped gaps between the top of the door and the jamb head may indicate structural problems.
◆ Check wallboard for loosening joint tape or popped-up nails; both are easy-to-fix cosmetic problems.

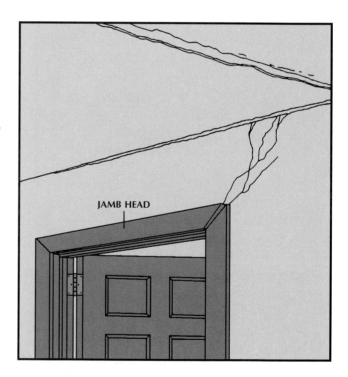

JAMB HEAD

Evaluating the Kitchen

✔Turn on all appliances to make sure they work properly; when checking the stove, test the oven as well as the burners.
✔Check the refrigerator-door seal for cracking and deterioration—both signs of age.

✔Examine the pipes and the floor under the sink for mold, rust stains, or other signs of dampness and leaks.
✔Turn on the faucets full force to confirm that water pressure is adequate and the hot water is hot.
✔If you are considering remodeling

the kitchen, make sure that there is enough space for new appliances and room for a convenient layout without extensive structural changes.
✔Look carefully at the flooring for damaged tiles or linoleum that will require replacement.

A hard look at wood floors.

◆ To detect tilt or sag in a floor, drop a marble or small rubber ball *(left)*. If it rolls repeatedly and quickly in one direction, indicating sag, inspect the underlying framing for rot *(page 112)*.

◆ Check for damaged or loose floorboards as well as squeaks, springiness, or window rattling as you walk across a floor—all signs of loosened subflooring or poor joist support.

◆ Inspect joints between tongue-and-groove boards: Gaps larger than $\frac{1}{16}$ inch or protruding nailheads will make it difficult to sand the floor for refinishing.

◆ Check for a raised lip at hard-to-sand areas—next to the quarter-round shoe molding or under radiators, for example. A lip $\frac{1}{8}$ inch high *(inset)* indicates that the floor has been refinished at least twice and probably cannot be sanded deeply enough to remove bad stains or lighten its color. Such a floor can only be replaced, covered over, or given a new finish.

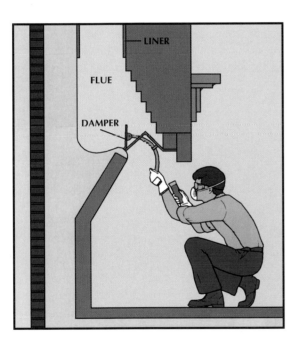

Inspecting fireplaces.

◆ Using a flashlight, make sure that the fireplace has a damper and that it operates easily and closes tightly.

◆ With the damper open, determine if the chimney has a liner and that it is in good condition, not crumbling *(page 68)*. A chimney that lacks a liner is unsafe.

◆ Inspect the front of the fireplace and the wall above for smoke stains, which would indicate poor draw.

◆ Measure the flue; it should be about one-seventh the area of the fireplace opening, and at least 8 inches by 12 inches for wood fires. Fireplaces that were designed for burning coal and gas have flues too small for wood fires; rebuilding is impractical.

Testing the windows.

◆ Note the type of windows. As a rule, wood-framed windows are more energy efficient and easier to repair than metal-framed windows.

◆ Make sure all window locks are secure.

◆ Look for windows that are out of square; such misalignment may indicate structural problems.

◆ Check the operation of all windows and look for broken sash cords, rot in wood framing, missing putty, and peeling paint.

Windows sealed shut by paint are not difficult to free *(page 58)*, but if windows are stubborn when there does not seem to be a paint seal, the frames may have settled. You will have to remove and trim the windows.

Evaluating the electrical system of a house involves determining whether the power supply is adequate, checking the condition of the wiring and whether it is safe for rated loads, and testing receptacles to see if they work.

How Much Power: The amount of electricity entering the house is measured in amperes (amps). Older houses might have a service capable of supplying only 60 or 100 amps—too little to operate a collection of power-hungry appliances such as clothes dryers and ranges, which require 150- or 200-amp service.

Check the amperage rating on the service panel; it is commonly printed on the inside of the door on panels with fuses, or on the main breaker in a panel with circuit breakers. If you see no rating, look for it inside the glass housing on the electric meter, which can reveal service capacity even if it isn't marked there *(opposite, bottom)*.

Older houses tend to have fewer circuits than newer ones, but an electrician can add additional circuits up to the limit of the service. For example, 150-amp service can supply as many as 30 circuits; 200 amps support up to 40 circuits. Note also the number and positions of electrical receptacles in each room. If some walls have no receptacles, it's a good idea to add some.

Examine the Wiring: Since most wiring is hidden inside walls, a complete inspection is never possible, but you can get a general idea of its condition by scrutinizing wires in the attic and basement *(opposite, top)* and near fixtures.

Turn off power to a circuit at the service panel and remove the cover of a receptacle or switch on the dead circuit to check the condition of wires inside the box; frayed or cracked insulation around the wires there indicates that new wiring is probably needed in places, though not necessarily throughout the house.

In some cases improvements in the electrical system must meet the requirements of modern building codes. And if you rewire part of the house, there is a possibility in some locales that the inspector may require you to bring the entire house up to electrical-code minimums.

TOOLS
Screwdriver
Voltage tester
Receptacle analyzer

Three-prong
  receptacle adapter

Evaluating a service panel.

Power enters the house through a service-entrance cable located at the top of the main service panel. It passes through the main fuse block—which cuts off power to the entire house when it is removed—and to the fuses to house circuits that exit from the sides of the box. The system is grounded by means of a bare copper wire that is clamped either to a nearby cold-water pipe at least $\frac{3}{4}$ inch in diameter or to a copper rod driven several feet into the ground outside. In a panel that contains circuit breakers, a main breaker takes the place of a fuse

block, and individual breakers control the circuits.

An old panel may be overloaded by modern appliances; if so, it poses a fire hazard and should be replaced as soon as possible. Signs of overloading include the presence of many 20- and 30-ampere fuses or circuit breakers, a burning smell near the panel, fuses that are warm to the touch, or darkened and discolored copper contact points under the fuses. A foolproof test is to compare the diameter of the wire in the circuit with the rating of the fuse or circuit breaker *(page 74)*.

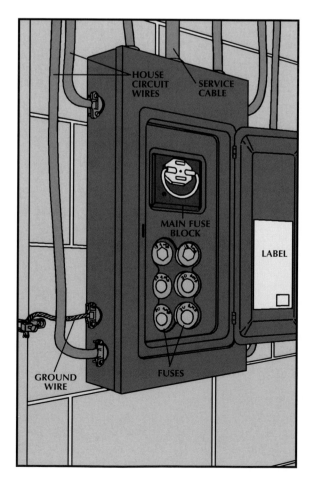

HOUSE CIRCUIT WIRES

SERVICE CABLE

MAIN FUSE BLOCK

LABEL

GROUND WIRE

FUSES

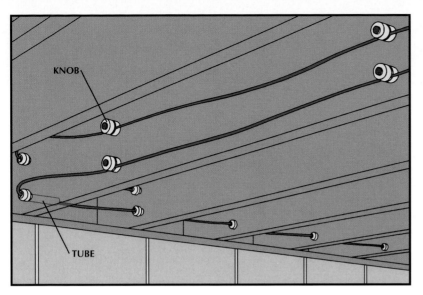

Appraising the wiring.
If the basement or attic joists are exposed, check the wiring. Outdated knob-and-tube wiring, illustrated here and identified by its paper insulation and the porcelain insulators from which it gets its name, must be entirely replaced. This old system is ungrounded and therefore unsafe.

With other types of electrical wiring, check the insulation for fraying or cracking; these problems indicate that rewiring is probably needed, although minor repairs are possible in some instances *(page 76)*.

Evaluating receptacles.
Test all receptacles with a plug-in receptacle analyzer. To adapt a two-slot outlet, remove the center screw from the cover plate, attach the adapter's ground contact to this screw, then plug in the analyzer and retighten the screw. Depending on the type of tester used, one or more test lights will glow if the outlet is functioning and safely grounded—check the manufacturer's instructions. If you find ungrounded outlets, consider replacing the first receptacle on the circuit with one containing a ground-fault circuit interrupter (GFCI). This tactic is less expensive than running new grounds, is just as safe as a grounded circuit, and protects all receptacles downstream on the circuit. Bathroom receptacles and those within 6 feet of a kitchen sink should also be protected by a GFCI.

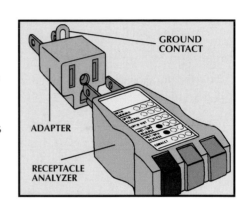

A Clue to Incoming Power

When all else fails, compare the electric meter outside a house with the photographs shown here to gauge how many amps the electric service provides. An old, 60-amp meter *(far left, top)* sits on a round socket that is barely larger than the glass housing. A 100-amp meter *(far left, bottom)* is fastened to a rectangular box little wider than the meter's glass bubble, while a 150- or 200-amp meter *(left)* is fastened to a box that is much larger.

Never break the seal on an electric meter or otherwise disturb it; the meter belongs to the electric utility, and tampering with it is a criminal offense in some jurisdictions.

TRICKS OF THE TRADE

Looking at Old Plumbing

The original plumbing in an old house usually includes cast-iron drainpipes and either copper or galvanized-steel supply pipes. Cast-iron drains rarely present problems—and if leaks do occur, the pipe can be mended as shown on pages 85 to 87. Copper pipes may develop leaks at weak joints, but the piping itself has a very long life span. Steel pipes, however, begin to clog with rust after about 30 years and do not normally last more than 50 years. Plan to replace steel pipes—perhaps gradually, starting with pipes that are exposed and any that are uncovered during other repairs.

A few old houses still have lead pipes. They, too, should be replaced. As with steel pipes, this can be done over time, but before settling on a gradual approach, have the water tested for harmful levels of lead.

Assessing a Well: If the water supply comes from a private well, be sure to have it tested for purity. In addition, check the well's storage capacity by turning on all the faucets and letting them run. If the water becomes muddy within 10 minutes, a larger storage tank is probably needed.

A Backyard Septic System: For a house that has a septic tank, ask to see the maintenance records. Intervals of 3 to 6 years between pumpings to empty the tank are normal; more frequent pumping implies that the system needs a larger tank. You can often recognize the leaching field, where effluence is discharged into the soil, by an area of lush grass in warm months or thin or melted snow in winter. The field must be on a lower grade than the house, and it should never have sections of standing water or mud or produce an odor of sewage.

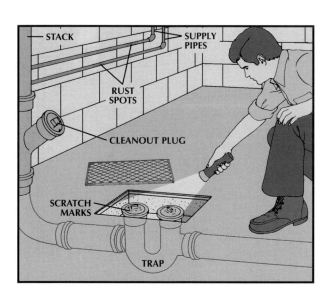

Examining exposed pipes.
◆ In the basement, locate the house trap or the cleanout plug for the stack and check for scratch marks from tools, indicating frequent removal to remedy clogging *(left)*.
◆ Inspect all visible drainpipes for signs of leaks or patching.
◆ Look for rust on galvanized-steel supply pipes. If it is confined to threaded joints, the pipes are likely to last a few more years; rust on smooth outside surfaces is a sign the pipes need to be replaced within a year.

⚠ **CAUTION** *Do not touch rust spots on steel pipes. You could break through an area that is weakened and cause a leak.*

Listening for leaks.
◆ Locate the main shutoff valve and make sure it works properly. A valve that is rusted open must be replaced. (Some houses have two valves, one on each side of the meter; check both.)
◆ With the shutoff valve open and all the fixtures in the house closed, listen for a gurgling or murmuring sound in a supply pipe *(right)*—a sign that a leak somewhere in the house is letting the water move.
◆ With the valve closed, listen for leaking in the supply pipe leading from the street main. If you hear gurgling, there may be a leak in that line.

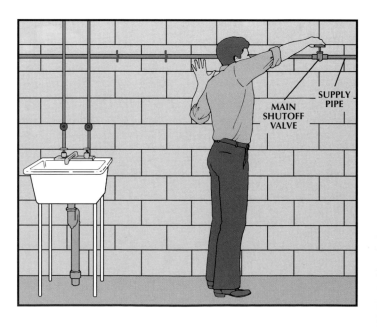

DISCHARGE PIPE

DRAIN VALVE

PLATE

BURNER

Checking the water heater.

◆ Look for a temperature-pressure relief valve at the top of the tank or high on the side; normally the valve leads to a discharge pipe. If there is no relief valve, one must be installed.

◆ Check the relief valve and the drain valve for dampness or drips. Leaking valves must be replaced.

◆ Look for other signs of leakage—corrosion on the tank, water stains on the floor, or rust under the burner of a gas water heater *(left)*. Any such evidence of leaks means that the entire tank must be replaced.

◆ Finally, read the plate that lists the capacity/recovery rate—how many gallons of hot water the unit holds and how many it can heat in an hour. In the case of a four-person family, a 40/40 rating is usually adequate for a gas water heater; a 40/50 rating is necessary for an electric unit.

Testing the water pressure.

◆ In the highest bathroom in the house, turn on the cold-water faucets in the tub and washbasin full force. Then have a helper turn on a faucet in the lowest part of the house. If the flow at the bathroom faucets loses a quarter or more of its original force *(left)*, supply lines inside or outside the house may be partially clogged, requiring replacement in 3 to 5 years.

◆ Turn off the cold water and repeat the test with the hot-water faucets; if the pressure drops again, the hot-water pipes—which run only inside the house—are also becoming clogged.

Inspect the caulking around the edge of tubs and examine the wall and floor tiles; deterioration can cause water damage in the rooms below. Loose tiles and cracked or missing caulking should be replaced as soon as possible.

Checking the toilets.

◆ Grip the rim of the bowl with both hands and try to wobble it *(right)*. If it moves at all, there may be a broken seal, which can permit leakage at the base of the bowl. Over time, such leaks can cause extensive damage to wood in the underlayment and subfloor.

◆ Remove the tank top and look for a date stamped on its underside; this is frequently a clue to the age of the original plumbing and therefore its probable life expectancy.

◆ Inspect the tank mechanism for corrosion, which may require the replacement of some parts. Flush the toilet to see how long recovery takes before water stops running and whether there is a strong swirling action in the bowl.

Reliable heat is essential, so always examine the heating system of an elderly dwelling before you purchase it. The challenge is to determine whether the system has life left in it or is nearing its last gasp. To begin, turn on the furnace *(see cautionary notes below and opposite)* and let it run for at least 15 minutes. Then inspect the installation as described on these pages.

Two Ways to Convey Heat: In most old houses, gas or oil provides the fuel for the system, and water or air carries the heat through the house. In a water system, a boiler heats the liquid, which then circulates through pipes as hot water or steam—either by a pump or by convection—to room radiators. Heavy cast-iron radiators retain heat longer than smaller finned convector units do, so a house that has both types may not be evenly heated because of this difference in heat retention.

In a forced-air system, air flows over a heat exchanger in the furnace, enters rooms through supply ducts, and recycles back to the furnace through return ducts. Feel for the flow of heat near supply ducts in all rooms, and place a tissue near return grilles; suction should hold the tissue against the grilles.

An oil-fired boiler.

◆ Look for obvious signs of leaking such as puddles on the floor and rust stains on the unit.

◆ Check inside the burner for a heavy deposit of soot—evidence of inefficient combustion—and examine the smoke pipe for rust.

◆ Turn valves and spigots to make sure they are not corroded.

◆ To find the unit's installation date, look for a service tag attached to the boiler or a nearby wall. Cast-iron boilers generally last about 40 years.

On a steam system, examine the sight glass *(inset),* which shows the level of water in the boiler. It should be about half full—slightly more when cold, slightly less when hot. Turn the valve at the top of the sight glass, then open the bottom valve for 10 to 15 seconds; if the sight glass drains but water does not continue to flow, the sight glass is clogged and needs replacing.

⚠️ **CAUTION** *Never turn on a steam-heat boiler if there is no water in the sight glass or if the sight glass is clogged.*

FLUE

DUCT

COMBUSTION
CHAMBER

A gas forced-air system.

◆ Start the furnace and remove the upper panel cover.

◆ After the burners light, hold a match near the flue to test for adequate draw—essential for complete combustion. In a properly functioning system, the flame will bend up into the flue *(left)*.

◆ When the blower starts, check the flames in the combustion chamber; they should be blue. Yellow tinges indicate incomplete combustion, usually caused by clogged or misadjusted burners. If the flames are slanted or wobbling, the heat exchanger may be cracked; the furnace must be replaced or repaired immediately to prevent toxic carbon monoxide fumes from leaking into the circulating air.

◆ Look for the installation date on a tag on or near the furnace: This type of furnace generally wears out in about 20 years.

⚠ **CAUTION** *If you smell gas around an unlit furnace, do not strike a match. Leave immediately and call the gas company.*

COOLING AN OLD HOUSE

Adding air conditioning to a house with a steam or hot-water heating system was once so impractical that the work was rarely done. Not only was there the formidable expense of ripping out walls, floors, and ceilings to install ducts, but the proceedings often altered the historic character of the structure.

Modern retrofit air-conditioning systems solve these problems. Designed with old houses in mind, they feature compact, flexible ducts that are about 2 inches in diameter. This airway is threaded through wall, floor, and ceiling cavities much as electrical cable is "fished" throughout a house, requiring only small cosmetic repairs.

Instead of louvered registers, these compact systems use round outlets, about 6 inches in diameter. Installed high in a wall or in a ceiling, they can be painted or papered to blend with existing decor.

Finding the Right Specialist

There are few improvements that a homeowner cannot accomplish with patience and careful planning. Although a professional generally can work faster, homeowners possess the greatest incentive to do a job well: They have to live with the results.

Nonetheless, few homeowners have the time, the inclination, or the tools to tackle every job, and some tasks should be left to a professional for the sake of safety—changing an electric meter, for instance, or connecting natural-gas piping. In these situations, turning to a specialist makes sense.

Before you do, consult the directory below. It lists the most common building trades and services, describes what these professionals do, and offers tips on what to look for in a contract with them.

Evaluating Subcontractors: Successful subcontracting depends on careful planning and thorough research. In considering potential subcontractors, first see that they are reliable. Find out how long they have been in business. If they are new to the trade, try to determine their current credit rating. Check for any complaints with a local consumer-protection agency or ask suppliers whether they pay bills promptly. A

bankrupt subcontractor can mean heavy losses for you.

Equally important are quality of work and the ability to finish it on time. Ask previous clients for references and, if possible, inspect the workmanship of past jobs. In many cases you can get sound referrals in your neighborhood, as it is a sign of good performance when a builder can rely on word of mouth to make a business prosper.

Whenever possible, secure more than one bid, but make sure you are comparing apples with apples. To do this, you may need to provide each bidder with a written list of materials and a description of the scope of work, as well as with copies of any sketches or plans.

Defining the Work: Once you have settled on a subcontractor, draw up a contract. Include your drawings and spell out—in writing—exactly what work is to be done, specifying the quantities, brand names, grades, and model numbers for any materials. Include a timetable for work and payments and stipulate that the workers clean up after the job. Finally, make certain that your subcontractor carries general liability insurance and provides workers' compensation for everyone employed on the project.

 Architect

Traditional contracts with architects give them full responsibility for projects and pay them a percentage of the total cost, but for renovation projects you may be able to find someone who will work at an hourly rate. On this basis, the architect can serve largely in an advisory capacity, helping you decide what to do, providing you with drawings, and recommending other specialists. But make sure that the architect's tastes and ideas are compatible with your own.

 Bricklayer

These specialists will repoint mortar joints, clean brickwork, repair stucco, and perform the heavier jobs involved in building or rebuilding masonry walls, fireplaces, and chimneys. Contact bricklayers early, because they may be hard to find during times when the weather is good.

 **Carpenter**

The versatility of carpenters makes their skills essential for any renovation work. Some specialize in rough carpentry: framing new walls and floors, reinforcing old, and building forms for concrete. Others do finish carpentry: laying wood floors, hanging doors, and installing cabinets and decorative trim. Experienced carpenters are often competent at both. Carpenters can often recommend other specialists and give scheduling advice. Most will use the materials you supply, but many get discounts at lumberyards and are willing to pass on the savings.

 Cement Mason

Check with these concrete or paving contractors when you want a professional to pour cement or to repair a driveway or sidewalk. You may have to make several calls; many companies are reluctant to do small jobs or give estimates.

 Contractor

Generally, you will save time and money dealing directly with subcontractors. But if you have a large number of complicated or interrelated jobs, a coordinator may be essential. General contractors will digest the plans, assemble a team of specialists, schedule their work, and see that it is executed properly. Some, particularly those who operate small companies, will allow you to do portions of the work yourself to save money. If you take on an intermediate part of a long job, plan to conform to the contractor's schedule.

 Dry-Wall Installer

Any careful amateur can fasten small pieces of dry wall to studs, but large sheets are unwieldy, and unless you have a helper, subcontracting may be the best way to guarantee a neat job. Many general carpenters will also do this work.

Electrician

Whenever you call in an electrician, you can reasonably expect the job to be done to professional standards. In most areas an electrician must pass a licensing examination, and electrical work must be inspected after the rough wiring is in and again after the job is completed. Most electricians will take small jobs or completely rewire an old house.

 ### Excavating Contractor

This subcontractor has the heavy equipment to do grading, trenching, or backfilling around a house, or even to excavate a basement or swimming pool. Many excavating contractors may be reluctant to take a small grading job, so checking with paving and landscape contractors may prove worthwhile. The latter prefer jobs in which they can sell you some trees, plants, or sod, but they are equipped to do grading around houses.

 ### Exterminator

Most exterminators will contract for a single job or for ongoing services with a renewable guarantee. The market is competitive; shop for the best price.

 ### Floor Layer

Professional floor layers work with carpeting, linoleum, and tile floor coverings and may specialize in one of these. Usually floor layers supply materials and labor; check the quality and price of materials as well as workmanship. This service is sometimes available through department stores.

 ### Floor Sander and Refinisher

This specialty is also performed by some floor layers and carpenters. Be sure to hire someone who does such work frequently, and always postpone floor refinishing until all other messy interior jobs have been finished.

 ### Glazier

You can easily replace small panes of glass yourself, but contract with a glazier to cut, fit, and install insulating glass or plate-glass windows, mirrors, and glass doors. Glaziers will generally provide both materials and labor.

 ### Heating and Cooling Contractor

Most heating and cooling companies feature a specific brand of furnace or air conditioner, so first determine the most appropriate appliance for your needs. Generally, the contractor provides all the equipment and oversees a crew of specialists—sheet-metal workers for air ducts, licensed plumbers or electricians for final connections. For repair jobs, ascertain the minimum charge for a service call as well as the hourly rates.

 ### Insulation Worker

Insulation materials come in a variety of forms—rolls, sheets, pellets, blocks, and pastes—and some contractors specialize in only one or two. In many areas the home-insulation business has become very competitive. Get several bids and familiarize yourself with the type, insulating value, and fire rating of the material each contractor is promoting.

 ### Ornamental-Iron Worker

Listings for ornamental-iron workers are usually mixed with those for heavy industry under "Iron Works." These specialists can fabricate and install, or repair, metal balconies, gates, fences, stairways, window grilles, and the like.

 ### Painter and Paperhanger

Some professionals do both, but painting and paperhanging are often considered separate trades. Most of the cost of either goes for labor, so shop for the best rate you can get for quality work. A recommendation from your neighbors is often the best bet—whether you are looking to hire a small subcontractor or a large firm that may be better equipped for exterior projects requiring scaffolding.

 ### Plasterer and Lather

Because most interior-wall finishing is now done with gypsum wallboard, locating a plasterer for interior walls, exterior stucco, or ornamental moldings may call for some detective work on your part. Ask local carpenters, general contractors, or the managers of old apartment buildings to make recommendations. Call a plasterer as far in advance as possible.

 ### Plumber

Like electrical work, plumbing work is regulated by code and licensing requirements. The plumber assembles and maintains any piping that carries water, steam, or gas, and installs and connects such household appliances as water heaters or dishwashers.

 ### Roofer

Roofers resurface or repair the outer layer of a roof to ensure that it is watertight. Some will work on the underlying structure, while others employ carpenters to replace sheathing or rafters. Select a recommended roofer specializing in your type of surface—asphalt, slate, tile, wood shingles, tin. Insist on a guarantee for a new roof; try to get one for any repair work as well. Many roofers repair gutters and will waterproof walls and basements. Some department stores contract for roofing and gutter work.

 ### Septic Tank Servicer

These specialists pump out and clean septic tanks. They frequently offer sewer- and drain-cleaning services as well. Septic tank servicing is available in most areas, for a single job or as a continuing service.

 ### Stonemason

A stonemason works with stone as a structural material in walls and chimneys and as a decorative surface for floors, patios, and stairs. You may have to make several calls to find a stonemason willing to do a small repair job.

Preserving Old Glories

After basic repairs are out of the way, it's time for the fun of restoring—and in some cases, uncovering—the age-worn details that make an old house unique. Using the techniques in this chapter you can bring new life to plaster walls and moldings, hardwood floors and trim, tired windows and doors, and a wealth of ornamental detail, from porcelain knobs to marble mantelpieces.

Restoring Fine Details   30

Quick Fixes for Porcelain Knobs
Refurbishing Interior Door Locks
Stripping a Flaking Iron Railing
Attaching a Loose Railing Cap
Resetting Iron Rail Posts

New Life for Marble and Leaded Glass   34

Patching Marble with Epoxy Filler
Silencing a Window Rattle
Replacing Cracked Glass
Bracing a Bowed Window with Steel Rods

Reviving Old Wood Trim   40

Working with Paint Removers
Special Tools for Taking Off Paint
Freeing Fragile Woodwork
Filling a Gouge and Shaping the Patch

Remedies for Failing Plaster   46

First Aid for Bowed Plaster
Large Patches for Walls and Ceilings
Restoring a Plaster Molding
Recreating a Molding Cast in Plaster
Shaping Running Moldings with a Template

Handsome Old Floors   52

Quick Fixes for Gaps and Holes
A Simple Brace for a Small Sag
Durable Patches for Damaged Parquet
Replacing Tongue-and-Groove Boards
The Right Way to Sand a Floor

Repairs for Balky Windows and Doors   58

Loosening a Frozen Window
Replacing Sash Cords
Reinforcing a Sash Joint
Making a Door Fit Its Jamb
Correcting a Sag in a Panel Door
A Primer on Pocket Doors
Curing Pocket Doors That Bind

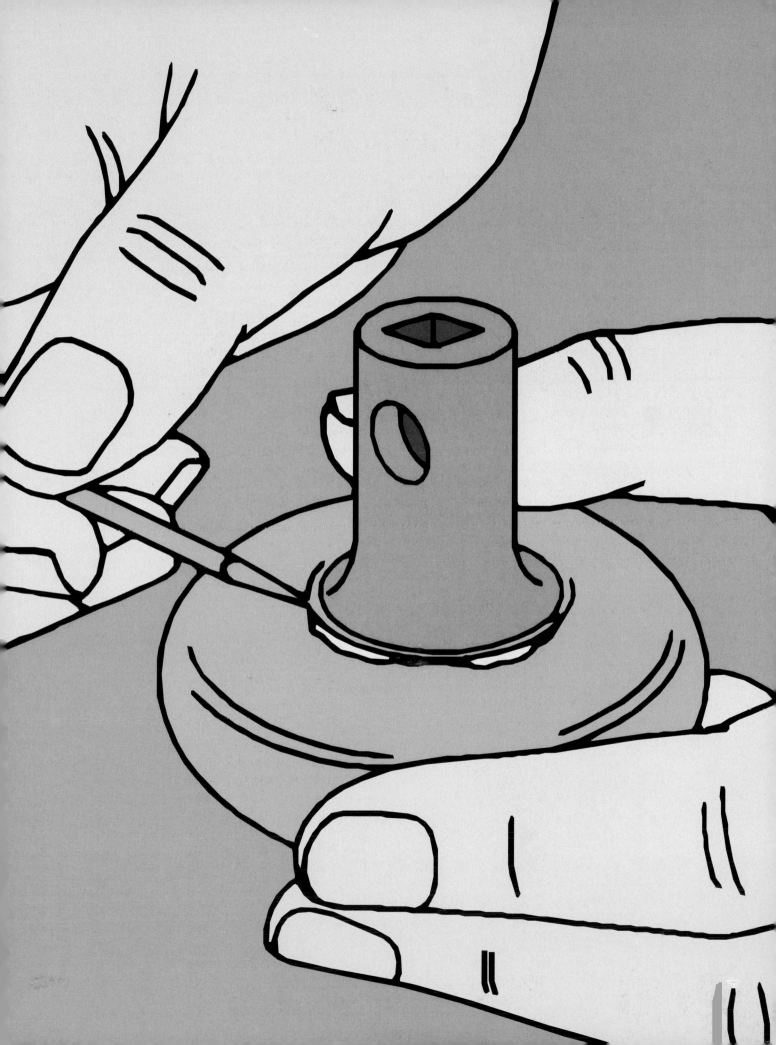

Porcelain knobs, surface-mounted door locks, brass fixtures, and wrought-iron railings are among the details that add character to old houses. These items often need nothing more than a little attention to transform them from shoddy to shiny—or, in the case of a shaky railing, from hazardous to helpful.

Rejuvenating Locks: Surface-mounted door locks are especially susceptible to rust. Although a rusted exterior lock is best replaced for the sake of security, cleaning and lubrication can often restore a sluggish interior lock. Designs vary, but the basic configuration is similar to that of the two locks on the opposite page.

Maintaining Iron Railings: Even a sturdy railing is likely to need refinishing to prevent damage from rust. Remove old paint and rust *(page 32)*, then brush on rust-resistant primer and one or two coats of an enamel formulated for exterior metal.

Some loose railings can be strengthened with simple repairs. You can reattach a railing cap with machine screws *(pages 32-33)*, and rust-weakened posts can be stiffened with metal sleeves *(page 33)*. More complex tasks, such as mending or replacing broken or missing railing parts, generally call for skill in welding and metalworking. Therefore, these tasks are best left to a professional.

TOOLS

KNOB REPAIRS
Toothpick

LOCK REPAIRS
Screwdriver
Tweezers

RAILING REPAIRS
Propane torch
Flame-spreader
    attachment
Paint scraper

Electric drill with
    $\frac{5}{16}$" bit and
    countersink bit
Wire brush
Center punch
Hammer
Ball-peen hammer
Cold chisel
Hacksaw
Adjustable wrench
Carpenter's level

MATERIALS

KNOB REPAIRS
Epoxy glue
Screws
Liquid paint remover
Porcelain paint
Emery cloth

LOCK REPAIRS
Lock oil

RAILING REPAIRS
Liquid rust remover
Steel post sleeves

Rust-inhibiting primer
Exterior metal enamel
Flat-head machine
    screws ($\frac{1}{4}$"), lock
    washers, and nuts
Stove bolts ($\frac{1}{4}$") with
    washers and nuts
Metal filler
Wire or cord
2 x 4s
Mortar mix

SAFETY TIPS

Put on goggles and rubber gloves to apply paint remover; add a respirator for products containing methylene chloride. Goggles, leather gloves, and a respirator are essential when you burn paint off metal surfaces. Wear goggles and earplugs to hammer on or around ironwork. Goggles and gloves are useful when you chip away old cement, and gloves are a good idea when you work with wet mortar.

QUICK FIXES FOR PORCELAIN KNOBS

A variety of knob repairs.
To tighten a porcelain knob that is loose on its metal stem, force a small amount of epoxy glue into the joint between the porcelain and the stem with a toothpick *(right)*.

If the screws that hold the knob to the cam are missing or worn, replace them with new screws of the same size.

Take dried paint off by covering the surrounding metal with masking tape, then wiping the knob with a paint remover *(page 41)*. Work outdoors if good ventilation is called for.

Apply porcelain touch-up paint, found in hardware stores, to obvious chips. Sand the chipped area with fine emery cloth, brush on a thin coat of paint, let it dry, and sand again. Build up the paint in layers until the cavity is filled.

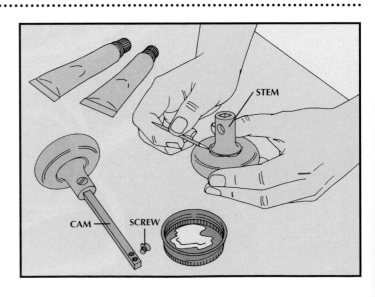

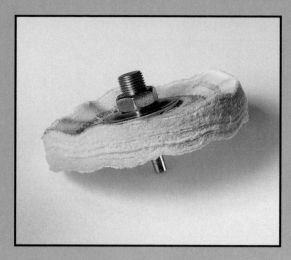
REFURBISHING INTERIOR DOOR LOCKS

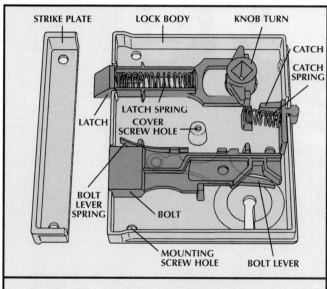

STRIKE PLATE • LOCK BODY • KNOB TURN • CATCH • CATCH SPRING • LATCH SPRING • LATCH • COVER SCREW HOLE • BOLT LEVER SPRING • BOLT • MOUNTING SCREW HOLE • BOLT LEVER

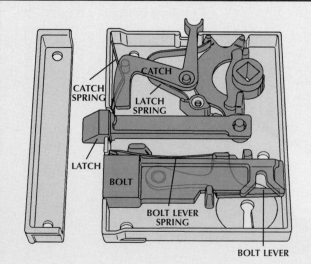

CATCH • CATCH SPRING • LATCH SPRING • LATCH • BOLT • BOLT LEVER SPRING • BOLT LEVER

Two interior rim locks.
The locks illustrated at left are mounted so that their strike plates are on the rim of the jamb and their bodies on the door face. Clean or repair them as follows:

◆ Remove the knob, then detach the lock body from the door by taking out the mounting screws.

◆ Set the lock on a flat surface. With a cloth covering your hand and the lock to catch springs that may pop out, unscrew the central screw that holds the cover in place.

◆ Sketch or photograph the lock. If you have two locks, leave one assembled as you clean the other.

◆ Without disturbing the parts, look for any that are broken, misaligned, or missing. In particular, locate and check the condition of three springs, which may be flat or coiled. One presses against the bolt lever and is operated by the door key. Another holds the latch extended. The third, a catch spring, provides tension for a small catch that can lock the latch in place.

◆ Remove all the parts of the lock. Have a locksmith replace any broken or missing springs. Other metal parts may be more difficult to replace or repair. A bent bolt can sometimes be straightened in a vise, but the force may break the bolt.

◆ Bathe the strike plate, body, latch, and bolt in paint remover, lightly lubricate all moving parts, and reassemble the lock.

STRIPPING A FLAKING IRON RAILING

Burning off old paint.

◆ Remove paint from exterior metal using a propane torch with a flame spreader attached. (A heat gun like that on page 43 also works, but not as quickly.) Direct the flame against a section of rail until the paint begins to blister.

◆ Point the flame away from the rail and remove the softened paint with a scraper *(right)*.

◆ Heat and scrape the rest of the paint.

◆ Clear areas where the scraper cannot reach using a drill with a wire-brush attachment, a hand-held wire brush, or paint remover *(page 41)*. Remove rust with a liquid rust remover.

⚠ **CAUTION** *Never use a torch after applying paint remover. If the paint contains lead, wear an appropriate respirator and follow the guidelines on page 10. Keep the area free of dry leaves and other materials that could be ignited by falling hot paint.*

ATTACHING A LOOSE RAILING CAP

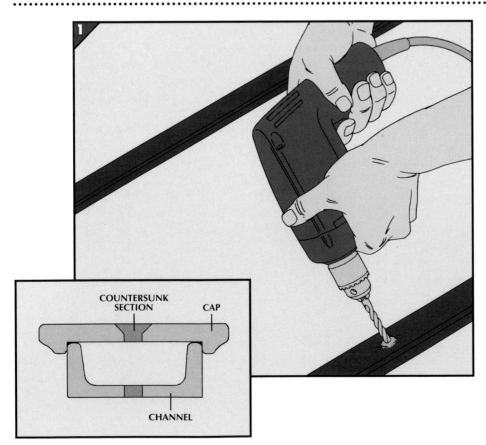

COUNTERSUNK SECTION   **CAP**

CHANNEL

1. Drilling the rail.

◆ With a center punch and a hammer, dent the railing cap midway between the edges.

◆ Using the dent as a guide, drill a $\frac{5}{16}$-inch hole through both the cap and the U-shaped channel beneath it *(left)*.

◆ After the hole is drilled, enlarge the upper end with a countersink bit *(inset)*.

2. Attaching the rail.

◆ Insert a $\frac{1}{4}$-inch flat-head machine screw into the hole.

◆ Slip on a lock washer and nut. Holding the head with a screwdriver, tighten the nut with an adjustable wrench.

◆ With a minihacksaw, cut off the screw below the nut *(right)*, then file the cut smooth.

◆ Cover the screwhead slot with metal filler, available in tubes at hardware stores.

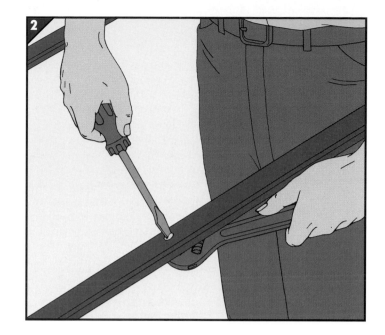

RESETTING IRON RAIL POSTS

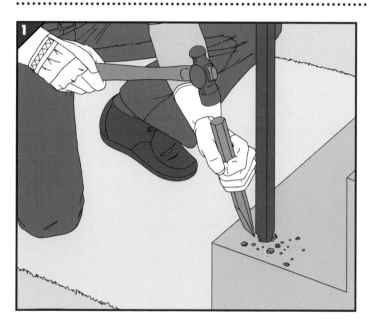

1. Digging out posts.

◆ To strengthen one rail post, you must dislodge and reinforce all of them. First, try uprooting the posts by hand. If that fails, chip away surrounding brick or concrete with a cold chisel and a ball-peen hammer *(left)*.

◆ Remove the entire rail, then enlarge the postholes until they are 1 inch wider than the posts and 5 inches deeper.

◆ Clean the post ends with a liquid rust remover. If the tip of a post has deteriorated with rust, trim enough from the post with a hacksaw to reach sound metal.

◆ Cut a steel sleeve for each post—round sleeves for round posts, square for square ones. Make each sleeve 10 inches long for each untrimmed post. For trimmed posts, cut a sleeve 10 inches longer than the piece you cut off.

◆ Slip a sleeve over each post end so the sleeve overlaps the post by 5 inches.

2. Securing the sleeves.

◆ Drill two $\frac{5}{16}$-inch holes, 3 inches apart, through each sleeve and post.

◆ Fasten the sleeves to the posts with $\frac{1}{4}$-inch stove bolts, inserting washers under the bolthead and nut *(right)*.

◆ Seal the joints at both ends of the sleeves with metal filler to keep out moisture.

◆ Set the posts in the prepared holes and plumb the railing with a level: Drive stakes into the ground on one side of the stair; brace the railing with 2-by-4s lashed to the railing with cord or wire and then nailed to the corresponding stakes.

◆ Mix some mortar; if you are setting the posts in brick, add brick dust to match the brick color. Fill the holes around the posts with mortar, sloping it slightly to shed water.

◆ Leave the braces in place overnight.

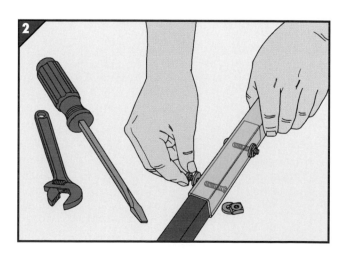

New Life for Marble and Leaded Glass

Marble mantels and leaded-glass windows grace old houses more often than they do newer ones. As the years take their toll in cracks, chips, stains, and sags, these materials sometimes need special attention.

Beware of Imitations: Before beginning any repair work on marble, be sure the material is genuine. In the 19th century, many mantels were made of dark-gray soapstone, cast iron, or wood, then marbleized—painted to look remarkably like the real thing.

To uncover such work, examine the back of a piece—scratch it if necessary—to confirm that the marbling is more than skin deep. If it is not, call a professional to touch up and restore the surface.

Repairs in Real Marble: Mending the severe cracks or breaks that occur in real marble calls for the skill of a stoneworker. However, a small chip on any horizontal marble surface can be concealed with epoxy filler, mixed and applied as shown on the opposite page.

Tightening Leaded Windows: In time, filler in the lead channels, called cames, deteriorates, leading to loosely fitting glass that rattles. To eliminate rattles—and also clean the glass and lead—refill the cames with a mixture of 1 cup turpentine and 1 cup linseed oil thickened to the consistency of pancake batter with plaster of paris. Stir in black paint-tinting compound until the filler is dark gray, and apply the mixture as shown on page 36.

New Panes: You can buy replacement glass for cracked or broken pieces at hobby or leaded-glass shops and install it as explained on pages 36 to 38. But in the case of older glass with ripples, streaks, or bubbles, some prefer to tolerate a crack rather than replace the piece with a modern mismatch. In this case you may be able to stabilize a crack by applying epoxy cement spread along the crack on both sides of the glass.

Bowed Glass: Leaded windows have a tendency to bulge inward or outward with time, as the cames contract and expand with temperature changes. Flatten a bowed window by weighting it down; steel rods reinforce the window to prevent future bowing *(page 39)*.

⚠ CAUTION *The solder for stained-glass repairs contains lead; work in a well-ventilated area.*

 TOOLS

 **MATERIALS**

 SAFETY TIPS

MARBLE REPAIRS
Hair dryer
Fine-tip paintbrush

GLASS REPAIRS
Stiff-bristled brush
Lead knife
Glass cutter
Vacuum with
   High Efficiency
   Particulate Air
   (HEPA) filter
Scissors
Grozing pliers
Soldering iron
   (80-watt)
Electric drill

MARBLE REPAIRS
Masking tape
Painter's whiting
High-gloss epoxy
   coating
Paint pigment
Hardener
Mineral spirits

GLASS REPAIRS
Turpentine
Linseed oil
Plaster of paris
Paint-tinting com-
   pound (black)
Epoxy glue
Sawdust
Tracing paper
Wood block
Sewing machine oil
Steel wool
Replacement glass
Noncorrosive flux
Wire solder (60-40)
Flameproof pad
Steel rods ($\frac{1}{4}$")
Copper wire
   (18-gauge)

Goggles are advisable for all the stained-glass repairs that follow. When you are silencing a window rattle, rubber gloves and a respirator protect hands and lungs from toxic chemicals. Gloves are optional for cutting glass; they can be slippery. If you don't use them, work carefully.

CLEANING STAINED MARBLE

Unstained marble is best washed regularly with a mild detergent. If a small area requires repolishing (a large job requires the special tools and skill of an expert), buy some tin oxide powder from a stone dealer. Wet the marble, sprinkle with powder, and buff vigorously with a buffing pad attached to an electric drill.

Stains that don't yield to detergent can be erased with a poultice—a paste usually made of powdered painter's whiting and a liquid chemical dictated by the nature of the stain. This paste is spread $\frac{1}{2}$ inch thick over the stain and kept moist for 48 hours under plastic kitchen wrap secured with masking tape. To finish, scrape off the paste with a putty knife and rinse the marble clean with water.

Organic Stains (Fatty): Caused by greasy substances such as milk, butter, hand lotion, or peanut butter, these stains require a poultice of whiting and enough acetone—nail polish remover—to form a thick paste.

Organic Stains (Nonfatty): These blemishes come from tea, coffee, ink, burning tobacco, soft drinks, fruit juices, flowers, colored paper or fabric, and the like. They usually take the shape of the object that caused them—the bottom of a coffee cup, for instance. Discolorations of this kind are treated with a poultice of 80 percent whiting, 20 percent hydrogen peroxide, and a few drops of ammonia.

Rust Stains: Orange to brown in color, rust stains generally take the shape of the metal object that caused them. Instead of using whiting, mix a poultice of powdered household cleanser and water.

Soot and Smoke Stains: Smudges of this kind can be removed with a poultice of baking soda and liquid bleach.

PATCHING MARBLE WITH EPOXY FILLER

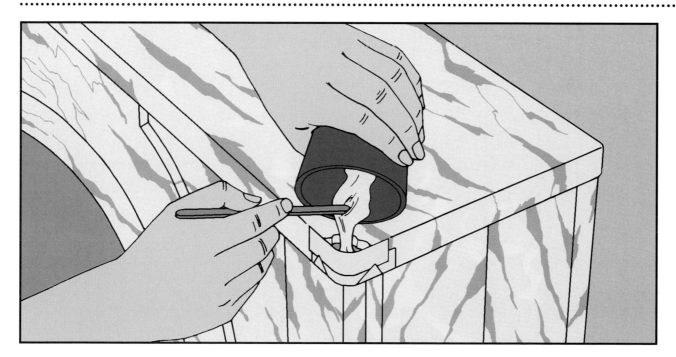

Filling in the chip.
◆ With a hair dryer, dry the damaged area thoroughly.
◆ Apply masking tape around the damaged place to make a form higher than the surface of the marble by the thickness of a couple of sheets of paper.
◆ Mix a small batch of filler to test the color. To do so, pour painter's whiting into high-gloss epoxy coating—used on many restaurant tabletops—to form a thick paste. Add paint pigment, available in tubes at paint stores, then hardener according to directions.
◆ Stir up a larger quantity and immediately pour it into the form *(above)*. Using a soft cloth, wipe the surface level with mineral spirits.
◆ To simulate marble graining, dip a fine-tip paintbrush in colored pigment that matches the marble and brush streaks onto the epoxy while it is still sticky.
◆ Remove the tape after the epoxy has dried.

SILENCING A WINDOW RATTLE

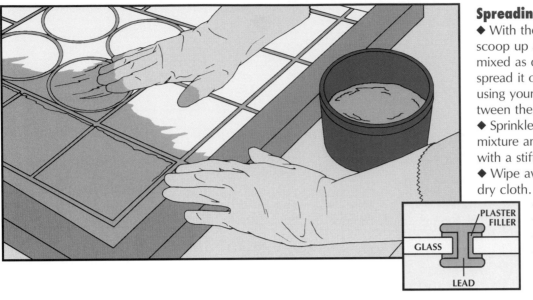

Spreading the filler.
◆ With the window flat on a table, scoop up a handful of plaster filler mixed as described on page 34 and spread it over the entire window *(left)*, using your fingertips to push it between the lead and the glass *(inset)*.
◆ Sprinkle sawdust over the wet filler mixture and scrub both glass and lead with a stiff-bristled brush.
◆ Wipe away the excess filler with a dry cloth.
◆ Allow the filler to dry for 24 hours, then turn the window over and repeat the process.

PLASTER FILLER
GLASS
LEAD

REPLACING CRACKED GLASS

1. Making a rubbing.
◆ Remove the damaged window. Decide which side of the window is looked at less, then lay the window with that side up on a worktable that is covered with cardboard or with several layers of newspaper.
◆ Lay tracing paper over the cracked glass and use a black crayon to make a rubbing of the full width of the surrounding lead cames *(right)*.
◆ Set the rubbing aside.

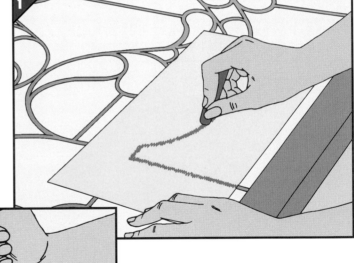

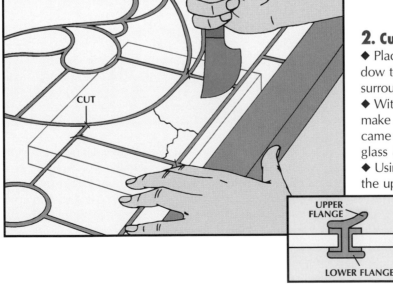

CUT

LEAD KNIFE

2. Cutting the came corners.
◆ Place a wood block under the window to support the cracked glass and surrounding cames.
◆ With a lead knife *(photograph)*, make a diagonal cut in each of the came corners surrounding the cracked glass *(left)*.
◆ Using the lead knife, gently pry up the upper flange of the cames to free the edges of the cracked glass *(inset)*.

UPPER FLANGE

LOWER FLANGE

3. Removing the damaged piece.

◆ With a glass cutter, score the cracked piece in a crosshatch pattern *(right)*, dipping the cutter in sewing machine oil for each score to avoid dulling the wheel.

◆ Set the window on edge, scores facing away from you, and, with the ball on the cutter handle, rap the glass firmly until it breaks out of the lead.

◆ Carefully discard all broken glass.

◆ With the tip of the lead knife, shave away old filler from inside the cames.

◆ Rub the came corners lightly with steel wool so the solder to be applied later will adhere.

⚠️ **CAUTION** *Since filler compound could contain lead, work outside on sheets of newspaper to catch debris. If you must work indoors, clean up afterward with a HEPA filter vacuum.*

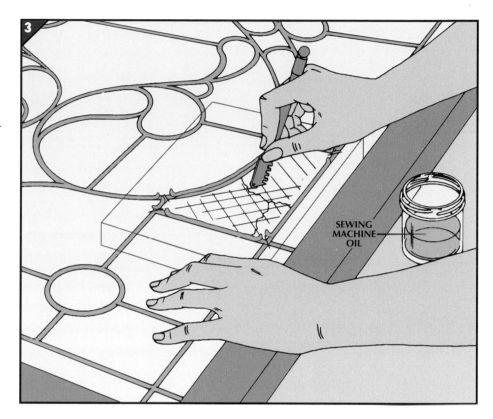

SEWING MACHINE OIL

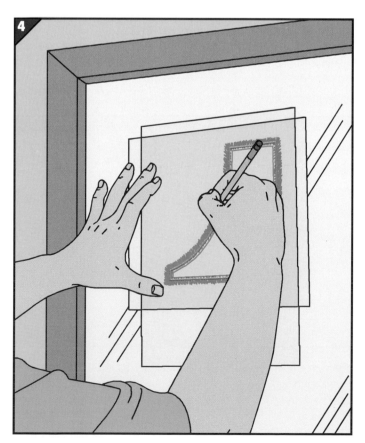

4. Preparing a template.

◆ Tape the rubbing made earlier to a sunlit window, then tape another sheet of tracing paper over the rubbing.

◆ Trace the inside edge of the rubbing with a fine-point pen or pencil.

◆ Draw a second line $\frac{1}{8}$ inch outside the first *(left)*.

◆ Carefully cut along the outer line to complete the template.

5. Cutting the replacement piece.

◆ Set cardboard under the new glass.
◆ Stick the template to the glass with a few drops of sewing machine oil.
◆ With single strokes of the glass cutter *(right)*, score all the way across the glass along the straight edges of the template. Use a ruler if necessary.
◆ To snap off waste glass, place your thumbs on top of the glass on either side of the score, make a fist with each hand below the glass, and twist your wrists so that your thumbs press outward to snap the glass.
◆ To cut curves, make a few gently curved scores outside the template *(inset)* and snap off the outer sections one at a time.

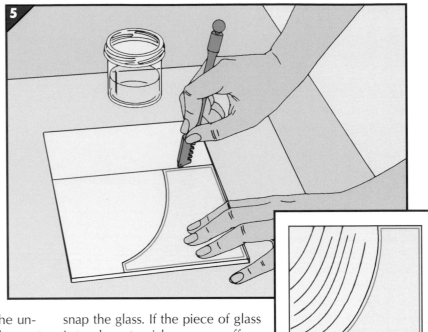

For glass that does not snap easily, tap along the underside of the score with the ball end of the glass cutter until the score becomes a visible fracture, then snap the glass. If the piece of glass is too large to pick up, snap off waste pieces at a table edge.

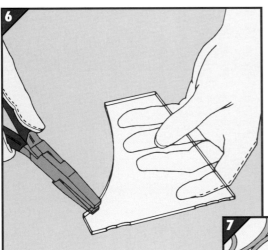

6. Grozing for a perfect fit.

◆ The new piece should slip easily into its place in the window; if it does not, note where it binds.
◆ With the tips of a pair of grozing pliers, nibble away bits of glass, no more than $\frac{1}{16}$ inch at a time *(left)*.
◆ Set the fitted piece back in the window.
◆ Gently fold the came edges onto the glass with the grozing pliers, then smooth the cames with the flat side of a lead knife.

7. Rebuilding the flange.

◆ To resolder the came corners cut in Step 2, apply flux with a small brush, then uncoil 5 inches of solder.
◆ Heat a soldering iron and coat the tip with a thin layer of solder.
◆ Touch the tip of the iron to the end of the uncoiled solder at each cut in the came, melting the solder so that it flows onto the came as shown here. (Solder that gets onto the glass can be cut away after it cools.) To prevent the glass from cracking, lift the iron as soon as the solder melts onto the came; set it down only on a flameproof

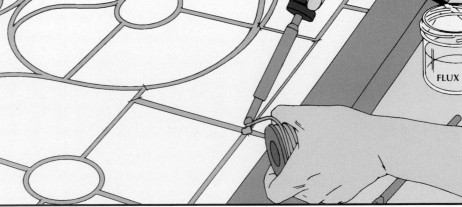

pad or in a holder. Clean the tip of the iron often by wiping it quickly across a damp sponge.

After the solder has cooled, apply plas-

ter filler as shown on page 36, at the same time filling in any loose spots along the cames of the entire window.

BRACING A BOWED WINDOW WITH STEEL RODS

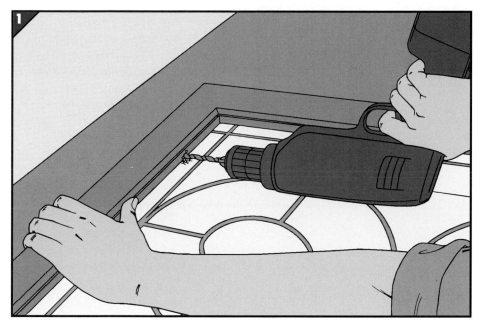

1. Drilling holes in the frame.
◆ Set the window on a flat surface, convex side up.
◆ For mild bowing, press on the glass gently with both hands. Cure a more serious bow with books. Start with one average-weight book per hour, up to four books in a day. Check after 24 hours; add more books if necessary.
◆ To keep the window from bowing again, bore pairs of $\frac{1}{4}$-inch holes $\frac{1}{2}$ inch deep on opposite sides of the frame, close to the glass *(left)*. Space the holes roughly 16 inches apart along the width of the window, drilling them so that the steel rods installed in the next step cross as many came joints as possible.

> ⚠ **CAUTION** *When flattening the bowed area, take care not to apply excessive pressure, which may crack the glass.*

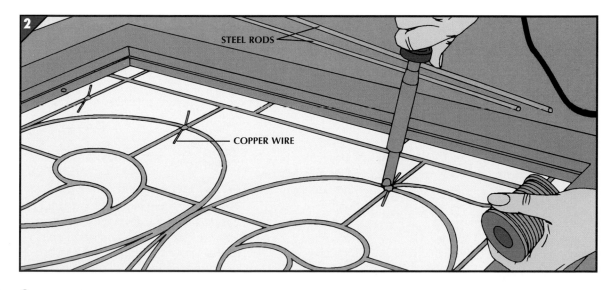

STEEL RODS

COPPER WIRE

2. Soldering copper ties.
◆ Cut a 4-inch piece of copper wire for every came joint that the steel rods will cross.
◆ Polish the center of each piece with steel wool and apply flux.

◆ At each of the came joints that is crossed by the steel rods, hold the tip of the soldering iron first to a wire in order to heat it, then briefly touch the solder to the joint to secure the wire *(above)*.

◆ Cut steel rods $\frac{3}{4}$ inch longer than the length of the window, then, one at a time, flex the rods and slip them into the holes.
◆ With pliers, twist the copper wires around the rods to secure them.

Reviving Old Wood Trim

Many old houses have hand-carved moldings, some made from hardwoods that are prohibitively expensive today. Too often, however, the condition of the finish conceals the trim's beauty: Dirt or age may have dulled varnished wood, or the carving's details may be hidden by layers of paint. The remedies range from a simple cleanup to stripping away old finishes and starting afresh.

Deep Cleaning: Wood trim that is stained and varnished may only need grime or wax removed in order to regain its glow. Start with turpentine or mineral spirits. Then, if necessary, use strong cleansers, such as ammonia, washing soda, or trisodium phosphate.

When cleansers prove inadequate, you can sometimes resurface the finish by quickly wiping on and wiping off the appropriate solvent. Use denatured alcohol that has been diluted with lacquer thinner for shellac, and lacquer thinner for a clear lacquer.

Paint-Removal Methods: Moldings covered by thick paint have to be stripped, partially or completely, to restore their original appearance. One option is to take out the trim and have a professional soak it in a chemical bath, but removing old, fragile wood must be done very carefully *(pages 44-45)*. The alternative is to strip the wood in place—a job that can involve hours of messy work. Old paint can either be loosened with a chemical paint remover and scraped off *(pages 42-43)*, or softened with a heat gun and then removed *(page 43)*. You may need to sand it to finish the job.

Consult the chart at right to select a stripping chemical. If possible, buy a semipaste version, which contains a wax that helps it adhere to vertical surfaces.

Partial Stripping: Only fine-grained hardwood warrants the labor of full-fledged stripping down to the bare wood. Many old softwood moldings have lovely shapes but undistinguished grains; they were meant to be painted, and the stripping job can be limited to clearing away enough of the old paint to reveal their detail. Use a heat gun to take off the excess layers, then apply a paint remover to smooth the surface for repainting.

A Full-Scale Job: If you decide to strip the trim bare, apply paint remover generously to clean out the pores of the wood. Patch any deep gouges *(page 45)*. If necessary, use oxalic acid or laundry bleach to remove stains that run deep. Spread the bleach over the whole piece with a brush and wipe off any residue with a rag. Bleach the wood repeatedly until the spots disappear.

After a light sanding, the wood is ready for a new finish. If you choose to keep its natural color, apply one of the clear finishes in the chart on page 42. Otherwise, refer to the box at lower right.

 CAUTION *Consult page 10 for advice on testing for old lead paint and working with it.*

CAUTION *Paint removers that contain methylene chloride must be applied in a very well ventilated area; do not use these products if you have a heart condition. Ventilation is also required when you use a heat gun or most removers, cleaners, and finishes. Keep flammable chemicals well away from any flame, including pilot lights, and dispose of oily rags in an airtight, flameproof can.*

 TOOLS

Paintbrushes
Molding scraper
Heat gun
Plastic stripping
  pads
Wiping cloth
Putty knives
Cold chisel or old
  screwdriver
Orbital sander

Electric drill
Sanding attachment
Hammer
Keyhole saw with
  metal-cutting
  blade
Pliers
Pin punch
Nail set ($\frac{1}{32}$")
Pack of playing
  cards

 **MATERIALS**

Turpentine
Mineral spirits
Ammonia
Washing soda
Trisodium phosphate
Denatured alcohol
Lacquer thinner
Paint remover
Oxalic acid

Laundry bleach
Sandpaper (medium
  to extra-fine)
Stain
Pigment
Japan drier
Clear finish
Vinyl spackling
Water putty
Wood putty

 SAFETY TIPS

Before stripping paint with a product containing methylene chloride, put on a long-sleeved shirt, goggles, a dust-and-fume respirator, and neoprene rubber gloves. Goggles and gloves are in order when you use other cleaning or paint-removing products, as well as most finishes. Wear leather gloves and a respirator when operating a heat gun; goggles and a dust mask are necessary when you operate an electric sander. Finally, put on goggles if you must pry away trim above eye level.

Choosing the right stripper.

Use this chart after determining the quality and condition of the wood in your trim. If you wish to strip fine hardwood bare, use a paint remover, chosen from the first three agents in the first column. To remove some but not all of the paint on softwood trim, consider a heat gun. To clean old trim, choose from the last two entries.

A STRIPPER OR CLEANSER FOR EVERY JOB

Stripping Agent	Use	Remarks
Paint Removers		
Water-base (various formulations)	Effective on lacquers, varnishes, polyurethane, and oil-base and latex paints. Better than other removers at extracting paint from deep wood pores.	Nonflammable, nontoxic, relatively little odor. Products based on dibasic esters (DBE) may require up to 12 hours to work.
Methylene chloride	Removes lacquers, varnishes, polyurethane, oil-base paints, and thin layers of latex paint.	Nonflammable, powerful, works in minutes, still preferred by many professionals. Noxious fumes; requires extremely good ventilation. Suspected carcinogen.
Methanol, toluol, acetone mix	Works on heavy layers of latex-base and oil-base paints, lacquer, varnishes, and water-base stains.	Flammable; use with special caution.
Partial Strippers and Cleansers		
Heat gun	Removes built-up paint layers.	Useful when wood is to be repainted; will not fully clean wood surface; requires some chemical cleanup; some risk of scorching wood.
Denatured alcohol	Dissolves shellac.	Can be diluted with lacquer thinner to cut back rather than remove the finish.
Ammoniated cleansers, trisodium phosphate (TSP), sodium metasilicate	Partially removes shellac, varnish, and water-base stains.	Can be diluted with hot water to vary strength; sodium metasilicate is a non-phosphate alternative to TSP.

GETTING WOOD THE RIGHT COLOR

The appearance of stripped woodwork can be surprising; raw walnut is not dark brown but has a grayish cast, and raw mahogany is not a deep, rich red but either brown or tan. Traditionally, moldings made from these woods were stained to deep colors. You can produce that effect with modern stains, simply brushing or wiping them on. The best stains are penetrating oils, which seep into the wood and do not conceal the grain. Some come as "one-step" formulations; others must be protected with a clear finish.

If you need to match the color of unstripped molding, you can mix your own stain. The traditional method is to experiment with pigments ground in oil, especially in these shades: burnt umber, burnt sienna, raw umber, and raw sienna. Mix the pigments with turpentine, then add 4 tablespoons of japan drier for each $\frac{1}{2}$ pint of stain. Alternatively, you can buy a few different shades of the same commercial stain and mix them to obtain the color you desire.

Choosing the right finish.

The first column of this chart lists the most commonly used clear finishes for wood trim, grouped in two categories: relatively hard finishes, which stand up well to wear, and relatively soft oil finishes, valued mainly for their appearance. If the wood is subject to heavy use, as with a chair rail or door casing, or may be exposed to liquids or high humidity, give special weight to the durability of the finish (column 2) and its resistance to moisture (column 3). If the wood is primarily decorative, make the clarity, gloss, and tone of a finish (column 4) the primary considerations. The fifth column of the chart deals with special problems of application and maintenance.

FINISHES FOR PROTECTION AND BEAUTY

Finish	Durability	Moisture Resistance	Appearance	Remarks
Hard Finishes				
Polyurethane varnish	Excellent	Excellent	Becomes cloudy with heavy wear; objectionable to some woodworkers for its synthetic appearance.	Must be roughened before recoating; generally incompatible with other finishes; water-base varieties have little odor and dry fast as you work.
Shellac	Fair	Poor	Available with a clear base or with a slight orange tint; polishes well to a high gloss; darkens with age.	Easy to touch up or to strip; dissolves in alcohol; do not use as a finish around a bar or wherever alcohol could be spilled.
Oil Finishes				
Tung	Good	Good	Matte finish, but can be thinned and buffed to a shine; wrinkles in heavy coats.	Not compatible with shellac; easy to refinish.
Boiled linseed	Poor	Poor	Prized for its soft sheen.	Recoats easily, coats other finishes well; poor base for shellac or polyurethane.
Rubbing and antiquing	Good	Fair	Can be rubbed to varying degrees of clarity or gloss.	Excellent as a finishing coat, except over shellac.

WORKING WITH PAINT REMOVERS

1. Applying the remover.

◆ Open the windows; protect the floor and other surfaces with cardboard. (Plastic sheets may melt.) Have scraping tools assembled and ready for use.
◆ Brush paint remover onto the wood with short strokes in one direction *(right)*. Back-and-forth brushwork would damage the chemical's bond with the finish.
◆ Let the remover stand for the length of time specified by the manufacturer, liquefying the paint into a sludge.
◆ Scrape the wood clean with a wide-blade putty knife whose sharp corners have been filed round. The sludge should come off the wood in a continuous ribbon; if it does not, brush on another coat of the paint remover and wait for a few more minutes before scraping.

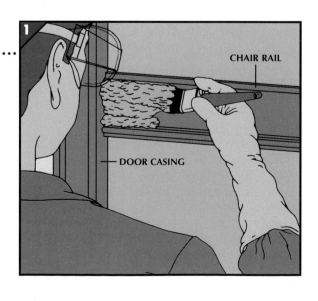

CHAIR RAIL

DOOR CASING

2. Cleaning contours.

◆ For grooves and corners that cannot be reached with a wide-blade putty knife, use a scraping tool with a contour as close as possible to the trim you must clean. A molding scraper, which has interchangeable blades that fit most common molding shapes, is one choice; see the box below for others.

◆ For multiple layers of paint, you may need to apply the paint remover again, waiting and then scraping as before.

◆ After the woodwork has been stripped, rinse it with the solution recommended by the manufacturer. Most paint removers can be rinsed with plain water or detergents, but some require a special neutralizer. Rub the rinse along the grain with a plastic stripping pad.

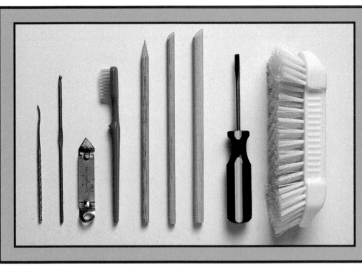

Improvised Scraping Tools

Instead of buying special scraping tools to strip paint, you can adapt household items to the job. Some tried and true implements include nutpicks, crochet hooks, church key can openers, old toothbrushes, screwdrivers, hand brushes, and dowels sawed off or sharpened like a pencil.

TRICKS OF THE TRADE

SPECIAL TOOLS FOR TAKING OFF PAINT

Using a heat gun.

◆ Cover the floor and other surfaces to avoid scarring by hot paint flakes.

◆ Set a heat gun at 700°F.

◆ Move the heat gun slowly back and forth, holding it 2 to 4 inches away from the surface of the molding, until the paint begins to bubble up from the wood.

◆ If the paint does not bubble within a few seconds, raise the temperature, but always work evenly to avoid scorching the wood.

◆ Scrape the paint away with the same tools you would use with a chemical paint remover (above).

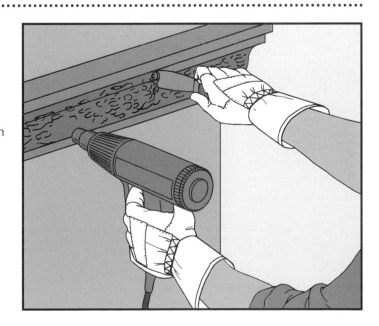

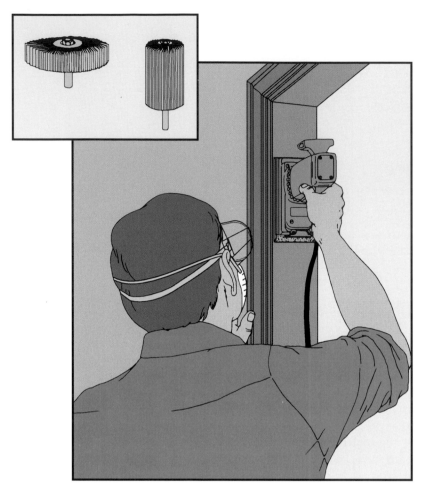

Finishing the job with a sander.

Sand away any remaining paint, adapting your method to each type of surface as follows:

Flat molding: Use an orbital sander and medium-grit sandpaper to sand traces of finish off flat molding *(left)*. Then sand by hand back and forth with fine sandpaper. Follow along the wood grain to remove any swirl marks.

Rounded surfaces: Sand these with an electric drill fitted with a large flexible-flap sanding wheel or a smaller flapped sanding drum *(inset)*; both are widely available at hardware stores. Do not use a wheel with wire flaps.

Small, concave areas: Glue a layer of felt around a small dowel, then hold sandpaper around it to form a sanding block.

FREEING FRAGILE WOODWORK

1. Loosening a brittle molding.

◆ Separate the paint joints between the trim and the wall, using a putty knife.

◆ Insert the blade of one putty knife between the wall and the piece of trim, then force in a second putty knife blade directly beneath the first.

◆ Lightly hammer a thin cold chisel—or an old screwdriver—between the two blades, loosening the woodwork slightly.

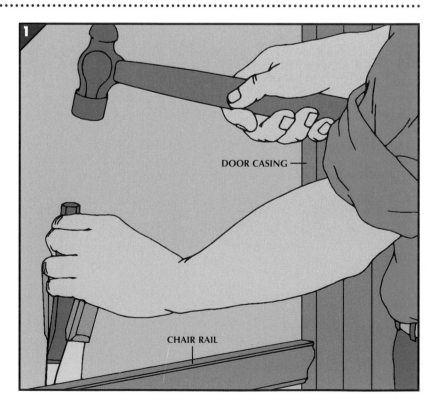

DOOR CASING

CHAIR RAIL

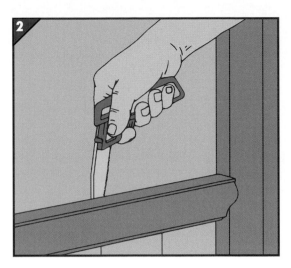

2. Cutting the fastening nails.

◆ To avoid marring the wall or the woodwork with further prying, use a keyhole saw equipped with a metal-cutting blade to cut the nails that are holding the woodwork in place *(left)*. Then gently pull the woodwork away from the wall with your hands.

◆ If you can, pull the nail stubs out through the back of the molding with pliers or tap them out with a pin punch *(photograph)* applied to each nailhead. Never try to pull nails through the front; you might splinter the face of the wood.

◆ As you remove the trim, pencil a number on the back of each piece; enter that number on a sketch of the room. Later, scratch the numbers deeply into the end grain of each molding; pencil marks disappear in the stripping tank.

◆ Lash long moldings to a 2-by-4 to protect them during transport.

FILLING A GOUGE AND SHAPING THE PATCH

1. Helping the filler adhere.

◆ Roughen the surface of a shallow depression by gently tapping a scattering of holes into the wood with a $\frac{1}{32}$-inch nail set.

◆ Select vinyl spackling as a filler if you are going to apply paint; use water putty if you plan to stain or varnish, wood putty for areas of heavy wear—door casings, window frames, and the like. Force a thin layer of the filler into the nail set holes with a putty knife.

◆ Build upon this layer to the wood's surface.

◆ Shape the filler closely to the contours of the molding with the edge of a putty knife or with your fingers, but leave at least a slight bulge.

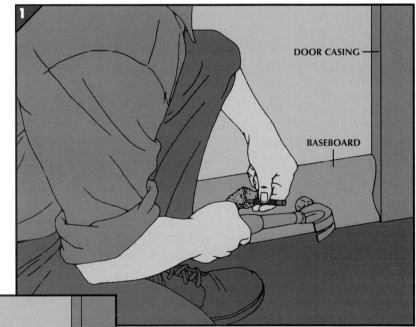

DOOR CASING

BASEBOARD

2. Sculpting the patch to shape.

After the patch is completely dry, sand it to shape with fine sandpaper. A sanding block formed by wrapping sandpaper around an old deck of playing cards, as shown at left, will conform to the contours of the trim and permit you to apply even pressure to the various irregular surfaces.

Remedies for Failing Plaster

Plaster, though durable, is a brittle material prone to breakage. Crumbling or water-damaged plaster must be removed completely, but other types of damage—in walls, ceilings, or decorative moldings—can be repaired.

Fixing Plaster Walls: Sometimes plaster sags away from its wood-strip backing, which is called lath. Plaster washers are often the simplest repair for bowed plaster *(below)*. Ask your hardware dealer to order some for you if none are in stock, or use $\frac{1}{2}$-inch fender washers as a substitute.

Cracks and holes may accompany bowing or appear for other reasons. Flaws that are up to a half-inch wide are easily fixed with vinyl spackling compound or with a fiberglass patch *(pages 97-98)*. Before filling a larger hole—one that is up to 4 inches across in a wall, 1 inch in ceilings—partly stuff it with wadded newspaper. Then moisten the edges and finish the job with thin layers of patching plaster or spackling compound. Because plastering large areas is challenging even for experts,

holes greater than 4 inches in diameter are best patched with wallboard *(pages 47-48)*.

Molding Repairs: Sections of plaster castings up to 10 inches long are easily replicated by reproducing an undamaged section *(page 49)*. Larger pieces are best left to a professional, but running molding—the type with smooth, continuous lines—can be replicated in sections up to 4 feet long *(pages 50-51)*.

Mounting a Running Molding: The completed moldings are cut to size with a wood saw and miter box. Construction adhesive and flat-head screws driven into joists or studs hold each section in place. (Brass screws work best; steel ones will rust.) Joints and screwheads are then concealed with plaster.

CAUTION *Before beginning repairs to plaster, check for the presence of lead paint and asbestos (page 10).*

TOOLS		 **MATERIALS**			🪖 **SAFETY TIPS**
Electric drill with screwdriver bit	Dry-wall knives (6", 12")	Plaster washers	Dry-wall screws (1", 1$\frac{5}{8}$")	Water-base clay	*Goggles and a dust mask shield eyes and lungs from plaster debris. A hard hat offers protection when you remove plaster overhead.*
	Pointing tool		Wallboard	Burlap	
	Watercolor brush	Flat-head wood screws (1$\frac{1}{4}$" No. 6)	Wood shims	Cheesecloth	
Chalk line	Wood chisel		Construction adhesive	Aluminum sheet (0.04")	
Utility knife	Putty knife	Wallboard joint compound	Joint tape	Lumber (1 x 6, 2 x 6, 1 x 2, 1 x 8)	
Ball-peen hammer	Pocket plane		Molding plaster		
Cold chisel	Tin snips	Fine-grit sandpaper	Shellac	Brads ($\frac{3}{4}$")	
Hammer	Awl	Plywood strips ($\frac{1}{4}$")	Motor oil	Wood screws (2$\frac{1}{2}$")	
Keyhole saw	File				
	Saber saw				

FIRST AID FOR BOWED PLASTER

Installing plaster washers.
◆ Mark the perimeter of the loose plaster *(blue lines)*.
◆ Drill pilot holes for 1$\frac{1}{4}$-inch No. 6 flat-head wood screws around the perimeter and in the center of the sag, spacing the holes 8 to 10 inches apart.

◆ Fasten a plaster washer *(photograph)* at each hole, tightening the screw until the washer is pulled below the surface of the plaster.
◆ Cover the washer and screw with wallboard joint compound, then sand, prime, and paint.

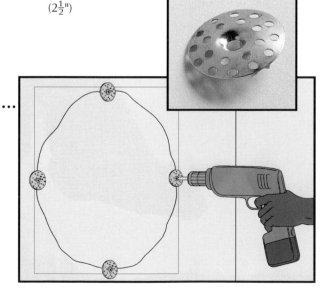

LARGE PATCHES FOR WALLS AND CEILINGS

1. Removing the plaster.
◆ On a ceiling, snap a chalk line to form a rectangle that encompasses the damage. Mark damaged walls in the same way.
◆ To protect sound plaster from damage while you are clearing deteriorated plaster from the rectangles, install plaster washers just outside the chalked lines *(opposite, bottom)*.
◆ Score the plaster along the chalked lines with a utility knife; with a ball-peen hammer and a cold chisel, remove the damaged plaster within the scored lines *(right)*.

⚠ **CAUTION** *When chiseling plaster, work in small sections and tap the chisel gently. Excessive force can loosen plaster beyond the plaster washers.*

2. Attaching plywood strips.
◆ Cut strips of $\frac{1}{4}$-inch plywood, 1 inch wide.
◆ Edge each opening with the strips, loosely fastened with $1\frac{5}{8}$-inch dry-wall screws driven partway into the lath.
◆ Shim the strips to position a scrap of wallboard flush with the plaster *(left)*. Tighten the screws.
◆ Trim the protruding shims with a keyhole saw.

PLYWOOD STRIP

SHIM

LATH

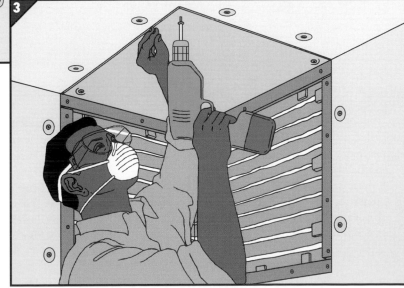

3. Installing the wallboard.
◆ Cut a piece of wallboard to fit each rectangle.
◆ Apply a bead of construction adhesive to each plywood strip, then press the wallboard against the adhesive.
◆ Fasten the wallboard to the plywood strips with 1-inch dry-wall screws 6 inches apart, starting at the corners *(right)*.

4. Taping the joints.

◆ With a 6-inch-wide dry-wall knife, spread a $\frac{1}{8}$-inch-thick layer of wallboard joint compound over all of the joints *(right)*.

◆ Embed perforated joint tape in the wet compound and run the knife over it, squeezing out excess material. Let the compound dry for 24 hours.

◆ Scrape off any ridges with the knife and apply a second layer of joint compound, called a block coat, with a 12-inch dry-wall knife centered on the joint. At corners, apply the block coat on only one side of the joint. Allow the joint compound 24 hours to dry.

◆ Coat the side of the corner skipped the previous day and wait another 24 hours for it to dry.

◆ On all other joints, apply a final skim coat of compound with the 12-inch knife, feathering the material to a distance of 12 inches on both sides of the joint.

◆ After all corners have dried, apply skim coats if needed—one side per day—to achieve a level surface.

◆ When the compound is dry, smooth all the joints with fine-grit sandpaper, then apply primer and paint.

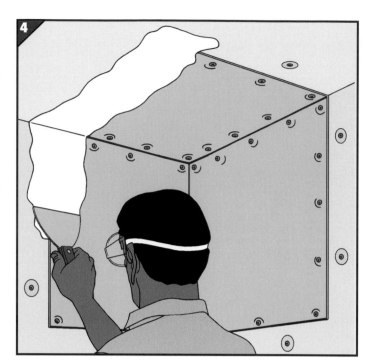

RESTORING A PLASTER MOLDING

Working with an ornamental tool.

◆ Dampen the molding; then, with the pointed end of a special pointing, or ornamental, tool *(photograph)*, press stiff plaster onto the damaged area a teaspoonful or so at a time *(above)*.

◆ For sculpting, use the opposite, flat end of the tool.

◆ Finish with a moist, soft-bristled watercolor brush to smooth the plaster, redefine the design, and remove any tool marks.

RECREATING A MOLDING CAST IN PLASTER

1. Making a mold.
◆ With a wood chisel, cut away damaged molding, squaring the ends.
◆ Select a section of sound molding with the same pattern.
◆ Dust the undamaged molding, coat it with shellac and let it dry, then brush on a lubricant such as motor oil.
◆ Press an inch-thick slab of water-base clay against the molding *(right)*.
◆ Score the back of the clay and spread on a $\frac{1}{4}$-inch layer of thick plaster. Before the plaster dries, embed a piece of burlap in it and add a second coat of plaster.
◆ After 30 minutes, carefully dislodge the clay-and-plaster mold.

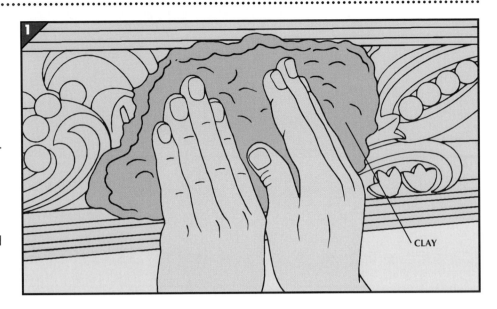

CLAY

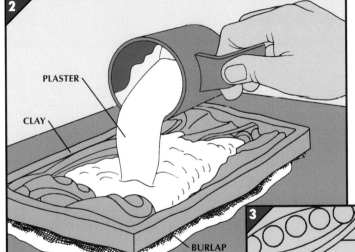

PLASTER

CLAY

BURLAP

2. Pouring the cast.
◆ Dam the ends of the mold with clay.
◆ Mist the clay with water and fill the mold halfway with a thin mixture of plaster *(left)*.
◆ Jog the mold, allowing any air bubbles to rise, then press cheesecloth on top.
◆ After about 10 minutes, fill the mold with plaster.
◆ Let the cast harden about 30 minutes.

3. Fitting the cast.
◆ Check the fit of the cast where the damaged molding was. Shave the back and edges with a pocket plane *(right)* until the cast slips into the space.
◆ With a utility knife, score the back of the cast and the wall where it will fit to help anchor the construction adhesive used to secure the molding.
◆ To the back of the cast, apply $\frac{1}{8}$ inch of adhesive, or more if necessary to set it flush with the adjacent molding.

◆ Set the cast in place and press it against the wall.
◆ With an ornamental tool like the one shown on the opposite page, conceal the joints between old and new moldings with plaster.

SHAPING RUNNING MOLDINGS WITH A TEMPLATE

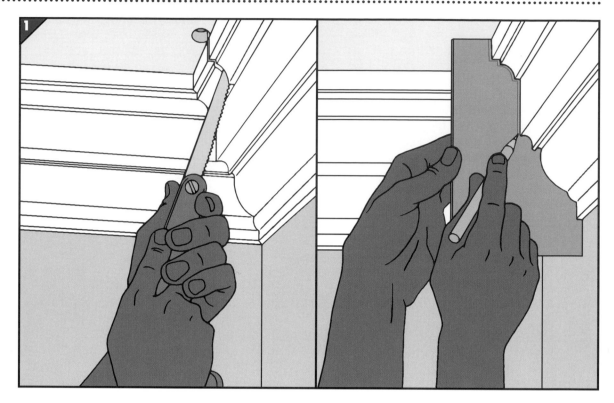

1. Tracing the profile.

◆ At one end of the damaged section of running molding, drill a hole in the ceiling that is large enough to accommodate the blade of a keyhole saw.

◆ Insert the saw into the hole and cut through the molding from top to bottom *(above, left)*.

◆ Slide a piece of cardboard $1\frac{1}{2}$ inches longer and wider than the molding into the kerf and, with a sharp pencil, trace the molding profile on the cardboard *(above, right)*.

2. Making the template.

◆ With tin snips, cut a rectangle of 0.04-inch aluminum $1\frac{1}{2}$ inches longer and wider than the cardboard.

◆ Tape the cardboard to the aluminum and place the assembly on a flat surface. Then transfer the profile to the aluminum by denting it with an awl every $\frac{1}{8}$ inch along the pencil line *(right)*.

◆ Guided by the dents, use tin snips and a file to shape the profile; smooth the edge with fine-grit sandpaper.

◆ Cut a piece of 1-by-6, 1 inch longer than the aluminum profile, then set the profile on it as you earlier positioned the cardboard on the aluminum, but with edges of the profile recessed $\frac{1}{4}$ inch from the edges of the board.

◆ Trace the profile on the 1-by-6, and cut along the line with a saber saw.

◆ Set the aluminum atop the 1-by-6, projecting $\frac{1}{4}$ inch on the profile edge, and nail it with $\frac{3}{4}$-inch brads every $\frac{1}{2}$ inch along the profile, every 2 inches along the other edges. If necessary, bend excess aluminum over the top edge of the 1-by-6.

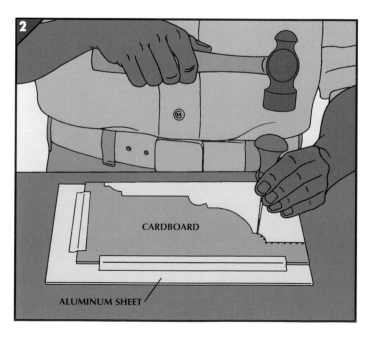

CARDBOARD

ALUMINUM SHEET

3. Securing the template.
◆ To make a jig to hold the template, cut three pieces of 2-by-6, 12 inches, 6 inches, and $5\frac{1}{4}$ inches long.
◆ Cut a 1-inch wedge from one end of the 6-inch piece.
◆ With $2\frac{1}{2}$-inch wood screws, fasten the short pieces flush with the ends of the long piece and offset $\frac{3}{4}$ inch above it.

◆ Set the template in the jig and lock it in place by driving the wedge cut earlier between the template and jig *(right)*.
◆ Check that the template is square with the jig, then attach a 1-by-2 brace diagonally from the outer end of the 1-by-6 to the end of the jig farthest from the aluminum template.

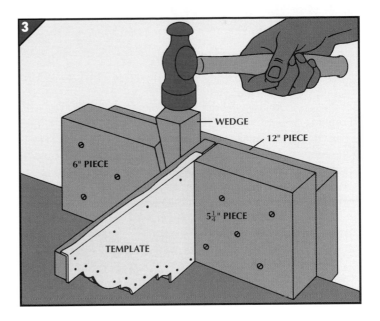

4. Preparing the table.
◆ With the jig snug against the front edge of the workbench, have a helper hold a board wider than the height of the template—here a 1-by-8—upright against the braced end of the template.
◆ Mark the 1-by-8's position on the workbench at 6-inch intervals *(left)*, then nail a 1-by-2 at the marks as a cleat for aligning the 1-by-8.

◆ Plumb the 1-by-8 and brace it against the cleat with three 1-by-2s nailed to the edge of the board and to the workbench.

Apply two coats of shellac to the work area of the 1-by-8 and the workbench, letting each coat dry, then brush motor oil on the board, bench, bench edge, template, and jig.

5. Making the run.
◆ Pour a $\frac{1}{2}$-inch layer of plaster—beaten to the consistency of honey for 1 to 2 minutes—on the workbench next to the 1-by-8, then push the jig along the front edge of the bench, checking to make sure the template's far edge remains snugly against the 1-by-8 during the run *(right)*.
◆ After each run, clean plaster from the template with a putty knife before adding more plaster for the next run.

◆ Fill any missed areas with plaster and make a final run.
◆ Allow 20 minutes for hardening, then score the end edges of the molding with a wood chisel and pull the new molding away from the board.

Old wood floors add character to a house and are often worth preserving. Restoring such floors to their former beauty requires sanding with special equipment that has been rented for the purpose *(page 57)* and then refinishing. Often, however, repairs must be made first. Fortunately, many of them, including silencing annoying squeaks, frequently require equipment no more forbidding than common hand tools.

Quieting Creaks: A noise can be addressed from either above or below, depending upon whether it originates in the finish flooring, the subflooring, or the joists.

Attack from above squeaks caused by finish flooring and some of those originating in a loose subfloor. Brush talcum powder or hammer small metal triangles called glazier's points into the joints between the boards. When these remedies fail, refasten floorboards with finishing nails or trim head screws driven through pilot holes and coun-

tersunk. The same technique serves to refasten a loose subfloor.

Other sources of floor noise require working from below. (If the ceiling under the floor is finished, take part of it down.) Wedge shims between the joists and any subflooring that has pulled away from them. Drive screws up through the subfloor to anchor loose floorboards. And install solid blocking or prefabricated steel bridging—diagonal braces that fit snugly between joists—to add stability.

Remedying More Serious Flaws: Other common defects in old flooring—sagging beneath small cast-iron radiators, wide cracks between floorboards, and holes left by the removal of pipes—can be repaired as shown at right. Do not neglect such repairs, as they correct genuine danger spots in the structure of a floor.

Extensive sagging is a symptom of weakened girders or joists. The cure, shoring or jacking up the floor, is shown on page 113.

Swapping Floorboards: Replacing missing, badly warped, or rotted boards presents no particular challenges if they do not interlock *(page 54)*. But tongue-and-groove boards—and especially those fastened directly to the floor joists without a subfloor—require special attention *(pages 55-56)*.

The size and look of old boards lend a floor character but make it difficult to find suitable replacements. One solution is to pull boards from inconspicuous places—closet floors, for example, or under rugs or furniture—and to replace them with new wood. Another is to forage among local wreckers and salvagers for old flooring. A third—and expensive—option is to custom-order duplicate flooring at a mill. Stain the new boards to match the old *(page 41)*.

⚠️ Floor sanders produce flammable dust. Seal doorways into the work area **CAUTION** with plastic, and ventilate the room with a fan.

 TOOLS

Chisel
Mallet
Sandpaper
Putty knife (3")
Post jacks
Electric drill
Electronic stud
  finder

Pry bar
Hammer
Nail set
Vise
Drum sander
Edge sander
Paint scraper
Tack rag

 **MATERIALS**

Cork stopper
Wood filler
Penetrating sealer
Felt weather
  stripping
2 x 4 lumber
Common nails ($3\frac{1}{2}$")

Linseed oil
Resin-coated nails
  ($1\frac{1}{2}$")
Flooring nails (3")
Finishing nails or
  trim head screws
  (3")

 SAFETY TIPS

Safety goggles shield your eyes while you are hammering or pulling nails, chiseling, or sanding a floor. A hard hat protects against injury from joists, girders, and exposed flooring nails. Earplugs or other ear protection guards against a floor sander's loud noise. Wear a dust mask to prevent the inhalation of fine dust and grit.

QUICK FIXES FOR GAPS AND HOLES

Plugging radiator pipe holes.

Wood plugs are the strongest fillers for holes, but corks are quicker and work satisfactorily in low-traffic areas.

◆ Pound into the hole a greased cork of slightly larger diameter.

◆ Chisel off the protruding end *(left)* and sandpaper the surface flush with the floor.

◆ Stain the cork to match its surroundings.

Dealing with cracks between boards.

Fill narrow cracks with either a wood filler chosen to match the floor color as closely as possible or a paste made with 4 parts sanding dust (taken from an inconspicuous part of the floor) to 1 part penetrating sealer.

For wide cracks, use a broad-blade putty knife to stuff felt weather stripping into the opening *(right),* filling each space to a level $\frac{1}{8}$ inch below the floor surface. If the weather stripping shows, pack the last $\frac{1}{8}$ inch with wood filler.

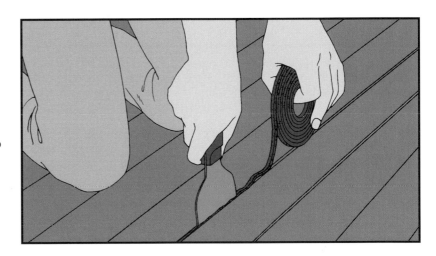

A SIMPLE BRACE FOR A SMALL SAG

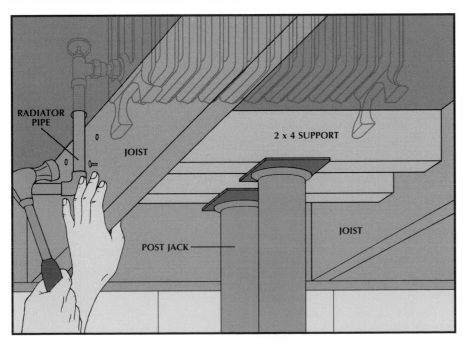

RADIATOR PIPE

JOIST

2 x 4 SUPPORT

POST JACK

JOIST

Installing supports.

Fix dips up to 30 inches long and $\frac{3}{4}$ inch deep by driving hardwood wedges between a joist and the subfloor. Level sags that fall between joists, such as those caused by a narrow radiator, as follows:

◆ Find the radiator pipes descending from the floor above. Use the pipes to determine the location of the radiator legs.

◆ Cut two 2-by-4 supports to fit between joists, and position them against the floor, directly beneath the radiator legs.

◆ Place a post jack under each support, then raise the jacks. As you do so, have a helper upstairs monitor the sag with a straight, 8-foot 2-by-4 or the factory edge trimmed from a sheet of plywood.

◆ When the floor is flat, nail through the joists into the ends of the supports to secure them *(left).* Remove the jacks.

DURABLE PATCHES FOR DAMAGED PARQUET

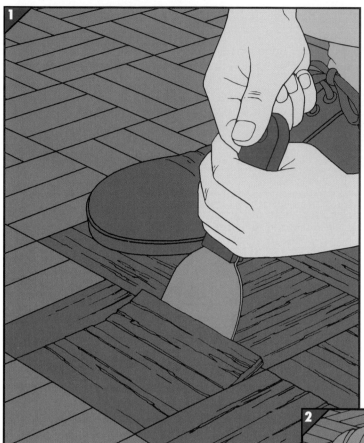

1. Removing damaged wood.

◆ For plain-edge parquet (without tongues or grooves), insert a 3-inch putty knife into a joint next to a damaged piece and gently pry it out, then use the opening to dislodge other deteriorated wood. If you have trouble loosening the first piece, move the knife along the joint, prying at different spots.

◆ After removing the old flooring, pull any nails that have worked through the wood and remain embedded in the subfloor.

On a parquet floor with tongue-and-groove joints, use a mallet and chisel to split damaged pieces down the middle, then pry out each half.

2. Inserting new pieces.

◆ Fit the new strips of parquet into place and tap them against the subflooring with a mallet.

◆ If the other pieces of the floor are face-nailed, drill pilot holes, matching the nailing pattern of the rest of the floor. Nail down the new pieces with $1\frac{1}{2}$-inch resin-coated nails.

For tongue-and-groove parquet, blind-nail through the tongue as you would for strip flooring (*page 56, Step 5*).

REPLACING TONGUE-AND-GROOVE BOARDS

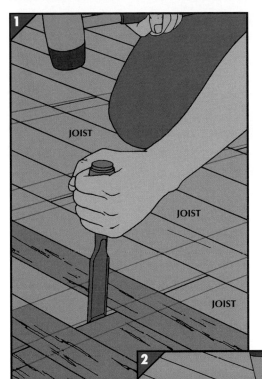

1. Freeing the floorboards.
◆ If there is no subfloor under the finish floor, use an electronic stud finder to locate the joists that pass beneath the damaged section. (Joists run perpendicular to floorboards.)
◆ Plan to remove sections of board so that the end joints of adjacent replacement boards will be staggered.
◆ In order to provide a nailing surface at both ends of new boards, chisel through old ones at the centers of joists flanking the damage. To do so, first turn the bevel of the chisel toward the damaged area and cut about $\frac{1}{4}$ inch vertically into the board

(left). (Where a floorboard ends at a joist, omit this cut.)
◆ About 1 inch closer to the damaged area, drive the chisel toward the vertical cut—or the joint between boards—at a 30-degree angle, bevel up. Continue this process until you have cut through the board.
◆ Repeat the procedure to free both ends of all sections to be removed.

Where a subfloor is present, you need not locate joists. Make the cuts as near the damage as possible; later you can nail floorboards to the subflooring.

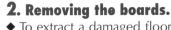

2. Removing the boards.
◆ To extract a damaged floorboard without harming the tongues and grooves of sound neighbors, chisel two parallel incisions along each damaged board as shown at left. Rock the blade in the incisions to split the board.
◆ Insert a small pry bar into a split at the center of the damaged area and pry out first the middle strip, then the groove side, and finally the tongue side of the board.
◆ Working from the center outward, pry up the remaining boards in the same fashion.
◆ Pull any exposed nails or hammer the heads below subflooring or joist surfaces using a nail set.

3. Cutting the tongue from a board.
To prepare a replacement board for fitting, chisel off the tongue where the new board will fit between two old ones. To do so, proceed as follows:
◆ Secure the board, tongue side up, in a vise.
◆ Make a vertical cut across the tongue to mark the section to be removed.
◆ Tap the chisel, bevel up, against the end of the tongue to split it off up to this cut.

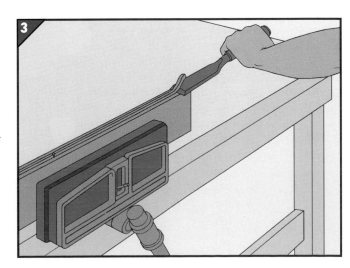

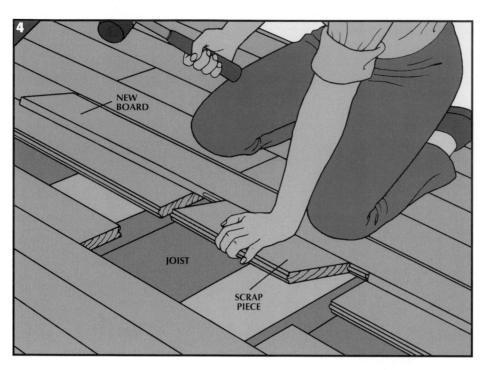

4. Inserting boards.

◆ To insert a new board *(left)*, tilt it so that the groove engages the tongue of the adjacent board.

◆ Fit a scrap of floorboard onto the untrimmed section of the new board's tongue and tap the scrap gently with a mallet to snug the board into place.

5. Blind-nailing a board in place.

◆ Drive and set 3-inch flooring nails at a 45-degree angle through the top corner of the tongue of the new board.

◆ Wherever blind-nailing is impossible—when you're fitting the last board, for instance—drill pilot holes and drive 3-inch finishing nails or trim head screws through the board, $\frac{1}{2}$ inch from the edges and 12 inches apart. Set the nails or countersink the screws and cover them with wood filler tinted to match the floorboard.

◆ To prepare the last board for fitting, lay it upside down on a piece of scrap wood and chisel off the lower lip of the groove as indicated by the blue line in the inset. Then tap the board into place tongue first, drill pilot holes, and nail it to every joist or the subfloor.

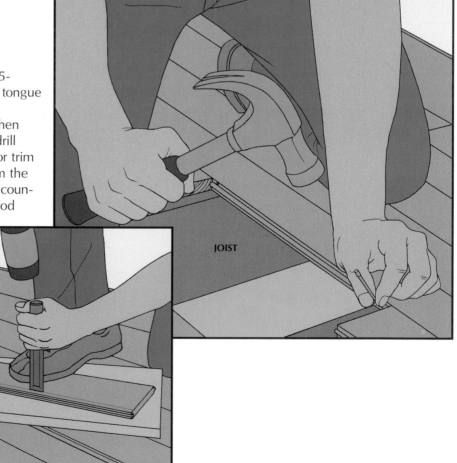

THE RIGHT WAY TO SAND A FLOOR

1. The first drum sanding.

◆ With the sander unplugged, load medium paper for parquet or herringbone-pattern floors *(left)* or coarse paper for standard strip flooring.

◆ Start at a corner of the room. Tilt the drum away from the floor, then turn the motor on. When the sander reaches full speed, lower the drum to the floor.

◆ Move diagonally across patterned floors and along the grain of strip flooring, always allowing the sander to pull you forward at a steady pace.

◆ At the far wall, tilt the drum up and swing the cord out of the way. Then lower the drum and pull the sander back over the area just sanded.

◆ When you return to the starting point, lift the drum and move the sander left or right to overlap the previous pass by 2 or 3 inches.

◆ Continue with forward and backward passes, occasionally turning off the sander to empty the dust bag.

◆ When you have sanded the entire room, turn around and run the sander along the unsanded strip against the wall.

⚠️ **CAUTION** *When the drum is in contact with the floor, keep the sander in motion to prevent ripples in the wood.*

2. The first edge sanding.

Use the edger, loaded with the appropriate paper for your floor, to sand the areas missed by the drum sander; the rotating disk of an edge sander can be moved in any direction on the wood.

◆ Repeat the drum and edge sandings, using successively finer paper for a second and then a third sanding. On herringbone-pattern or parquet floors, do the second drum sanding on the opposite diagonal to the first, and do the final sanding along the length of the room *(inset, top)*. On standard strip floors move the drum sander along the grain for each sanding *(inset, bottom)*.

◆ Remove old finish under radiators, in corners, and in other tight spots by working along the grain with a sharp paint scraper. Sand these areas by hand.

◆ To clean up, first vacuum the ceiling, walls, and floor, paying particular attention to all edges and corners. Then pick up fine dust using either a dust mop dampened with linseed oil if you plan to varnish, or a tack rag if you plan to apply polyurethane.

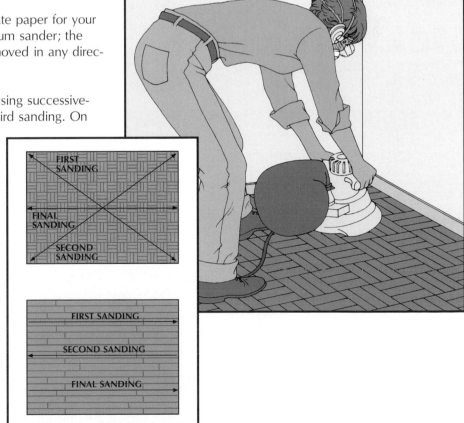

Doors and windows are among the most vulnerable parts of a house: They are often exposed to the ravages of the weather; constant use wears out their hardware; and moisture and age cause them to warp, sag, and swell.

Balky Windows: Most older houses have double-hung windows. All too often the sashes bind or they are frozen shut by layers of paint. Or sash cords—especially the lower ones—break, resulting in windows that won't stay open. When replacing a broken cord on one side of a window, renew the other cord as well. If your windows have metal pulleys with wide grooves, you can replace the cords with indestructible metal sash chains.

Doors That Bind: When a door sticks or drags, first check for loose hinges. If the screw holes are stripped, glue in wood dowels and redrill the screw holes. Shimming the hinges or planing the door edge may be in order if the house has settled and the doorframe is no longer square. Where the frame is square but the door is not, you can realign the door.

Pocket doors, which disappear into walls and roll either on the floor or on overhead tracks, have special difficulties. Diagnosis of a problem is complicated by a bewildering variety of construction methods. If the repairs shown on pages 64 to 65 fail, the only solution is to remove a section of the wall to get at the trouble.

Working with Wood and Plaster: Moisture swells unsealed wood, so a sash or door planed in humid weather is likely to become loose during the winter. The best time to repair windows and doors is during a dry season; seal planed or sanded edges with paint or varnish as soon as possible after you fix the door.

When working with window or door casings or repairing a pocket door, remember that old materials are brittle. Remove wood moldings with care, and avoid jarring the walls, which could shake plaster loose from its lath.

 Building materials often contain lead and asbestos; **CAUTION** *check the precautions on page 10.*

 TOOLS

Window opener
Hammer
Pry bar
1" paint scraper
Long-nose pliers
Carpenter's
  nippers
Wire brush
Bar clamp
Electric drill

Drill bits
  ($\frac{5}{16}$" and $\frac{1}{2}$")
Drum-rasp drill
  attachment
Drill guide
Mallet
Wood chisel
Screwdriver
Block plane
Jack plane
Putty knife

 MATERIALS

Scrap lumber
2 x 4
Sandpaper
Paraffin
Sash cord or chain
Finishing nails ($1\frac{1}{4}$")
Fluted dowels
  ($\frac{5}{16}$" and $\frac{1}{2}$")

Wood glue
Cardboard
Metal washers
Lipstick
Plywood sheet
Wood putty
Metal screw eyes
Heavy-gauge wire
Wood screws
  ($1\frac{1}{2}$" No. 6)

SAFETY TIPS

To protect against dust and splinters when repairing old doors and windows, consider wearing gloves and a dust mask. Add goggles when working at eye level or higher and when using a drum rasp.

LOOSENING A FROZEN WINDOW

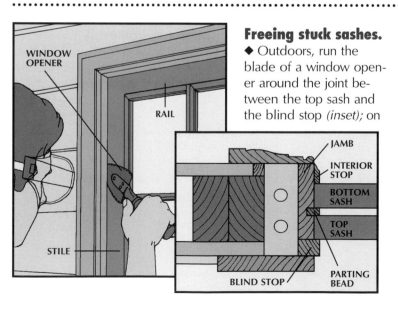

WINDOW OPENER
RAIL
STILE
JAMB
INTERIOR STOP
BOTTOM SASH
TOP SASH
BLIND STOP
PARTING BEAD

Freeing stuck sashes.
◆ Outdoors, run the blade of a window opener around the joint between the top sash and the blind stop *(inset);* on the bottom sash, insert the blade between the sash and the parting bead.
◆ Inside, run the window opener between the top sash and the parting bead, and between the bottom sash and the interior stop.

◆ If the bottom sash remains frozen, place a wood block at one end of the outside sill. Wedge a pry bar between the block and the rail, directly under the stile. Carefully pry the sash up, al-ternating from one side of the window to the other.
◆ On the top sash, pry out the top blind stop, adapting the techniques on pages 44 and 45. Wedge the pry bar between the top rail and a block of wood placed in the corner of the jamb, and pry the sash down.

 Pry only at the ends of rails; **CAUTION** *pressure elsewhere could cause a windowpane to break.*

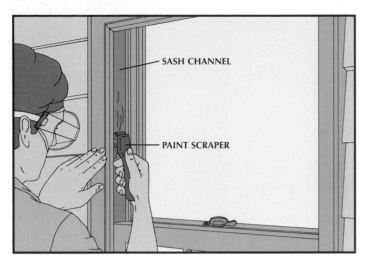

Easing a tight sash channel.
◆ Use a 1-inch paint scraper to pare paint and dirt from the sash channels, including the stops and parting bead.
◆ Sand the channels smooth, using a wood sanding block slightly narrower than the channel, then lubricate the channels with a block of household paraffin.

REPLACING SASH CORDS

1. Removing a bottom sash.
◆ Remove the interior stop on one side of the window.
◆ Raise the sash slightly and angle its side free of the jamb, then rest the sash on the window sill.
◆ Grip the knot in the end of the broken cord with long-nose pliers and pull it out of the sash.
◆ Untie the knot on the other side of the sash and set the sash aside.
◆ On a window with access plates *(inset),* remove the screws or nails that secure the plates and pry them out; if necessary, remove the parting bead to get at a plate. On a window without ac-

cess plates, remove the casings that conceal the sash weights.
◆ Retrieve the weights from the bottom of the window frame and untie the cords.

If the window has interlocking weather stripping—the metal type that fits into a groove in the sash—remove it when you pull out the sash. To do so, raise the sash to the top of the frame and use carpenter's nippers to remove the nails that fasten the weather stripping track. Lower the sash and remove it—along with the weather stripping.

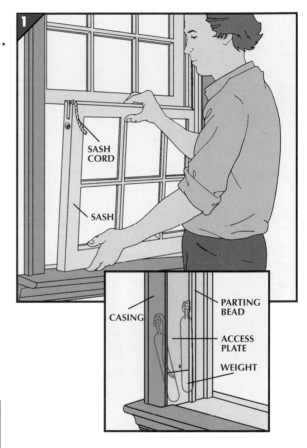

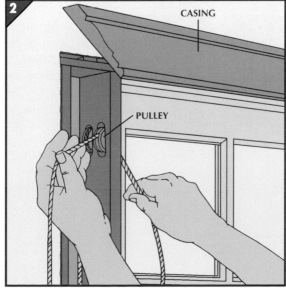

2. Threading new cords.
For a window with no access plate, knot a new cord to a counterweight at a point about 3 inches from one end of the cord. Feed the other end over the pulley *(left).* Repeat with the second cord.

For a window with access plates, tie a piece of string to a bent nail and feed the nail and string over the pulley until the nail appears at the access hole; then tie the other end of the string to the sash cord. Use the string to pull the cord down, and tie the cord to the weight. Repeat with the second cord.

3. Adjusting the cords.

◆ Set the sash on the sill.
◆ Thread the cord through its slot in the edge of the sash.
◆ Pull the cord to raise the weight to the pulley, then lower the weight about 2 inches. Knot the cord and trim it close to the knot.
◆ Repeat with the second cord.
◆ Set the sash in its channel, raise it to the top of the frame, and check that the weights are suspended about 2 inches from the bottom of the compartment. Adjust the cords as needed.
◆ Replace the casing or access plate, then fasten the stop with $1\frac{1}{4}$-inch finishing nails.

REINFORCING A SASH JOINT

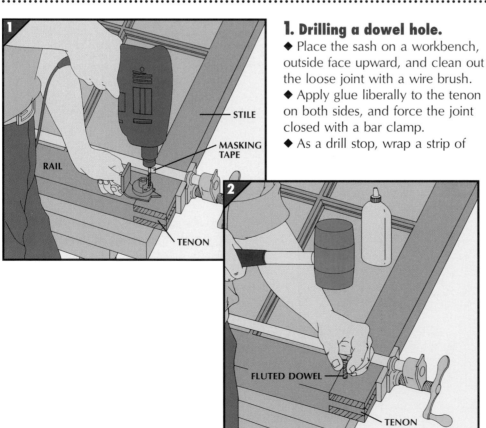

1. Drilling a dowel hole.

◆ Place the sash on a workbench, outside face upward, and clean out the loose joint with a wire brush.
◆ Apply glue liberally to the tenon on both sides, and force the joint closed with a bar clamp.
◆ As a drill stop, wrap a strip of masking tape around a $\frac{5}{16}$-inch bit. Position the tape $\frac{1}{8}$ inch nearer the bit's tip than the sash's thickness.
◆ Place a drill guide on the stile, at the center of the rail and $\frac{1}{2}$ inch from the joint. Drill the hole, stopping when the masking tape hits the drill guide.

2. Pinning the tenon.

◆ Cut a $\frac{5}{16}$-inch fluted wood dowel slightly longer than the depth of the hole.
◆ Coat the dowel with wood glue, tap it into the hole with a mallet, and let the glue dry overnight.
◆ Chisel the end of the dowel flush with the face of the sash.
◆ Sand the surface smooth, then paint the window.

A door that scrapes the floor.

◆ For a two-knuckle hinge *(right)*, lift the door off the hinge pins and slide washers onto the pins of both hinges.

◆ Experiment with washers of different thicknesses until the door no longer scrapes; the thickness of each set of washers should not exceed $\frac{1}{8}$ inch.

◆ For a hinge with interlocking knuckles and removable pins *(inset)*, remove the screws fastening the lower hinge to the jamb, and wedge the bottom of the door up slightly.

◆ Cut a cardboard shim and slide it behind the hinge leaf.

◆ Experiment to find the correct shim thickness, then replace the screws.

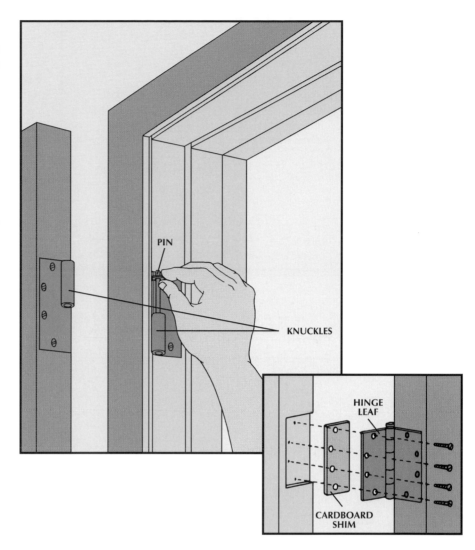

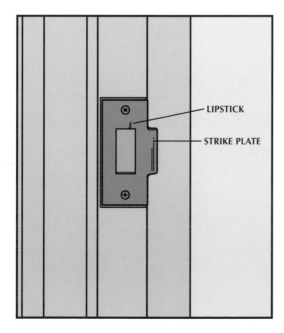

A door that will not latch.

◆ Cover the tip of the latch bolt with dark lipstick.

◆ With the doorknob turned to hold the latch bolt open, close the door, then release the knob. Turn the knob again to retract the bolt and open the door.

◆ If the imprint of the lipstick is more than $\frac{1}{4}$ inch out of line with the hole in the strike plate, remove the strike plate.

◆ Tape a piece of paper over the mortise, then repeat the steps above to mark the latch bolt's position on the paper.

◆ Align the strike plate with the imprint and mark around it for a new mortise and bolt hole, then enlarge the mortise and bolt hole with a wood chisel.

◆ Replace the strike plate and fill the exposed portions of the old mortise with wood filler.

If the imprint is less than $\frac{1}{4}$ inch off, clamp the strike plate in a vise and enlarge the strike opening with a file; do not enlarge the mortise.

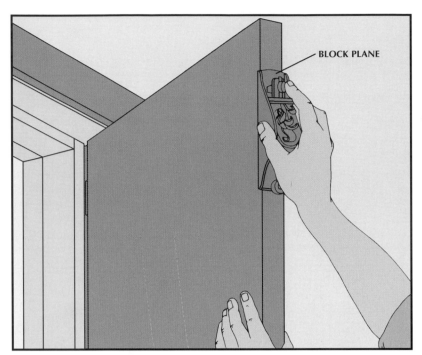

Freeing a door that binds.

For a minor problem, tap a wedge beneath the door to hold it open, then use a block plane to gradually pare the edge that binds, until the gap between the door and jamb is even.

◆ If an entire edge binds on the strike or hinge side, remove the door and unscrew the hinges.
◆ Mark a line $\frac{1}{8}$ inch from the hinge edge on both sides of the door and have a helper hold the door while you plane down to the lines with a jack plane.
◆ Test the fit of the door and mark any points that require additional planing.
◆ Widen the hinge mortises before reattaching the hinges, then rehang the door.

⚠ **CAUTION** *To avoid splintering when planing the top or bottom of a door, always work from a corner toward the center.*

CORRECTING A SAG IN A PANEL DOOR

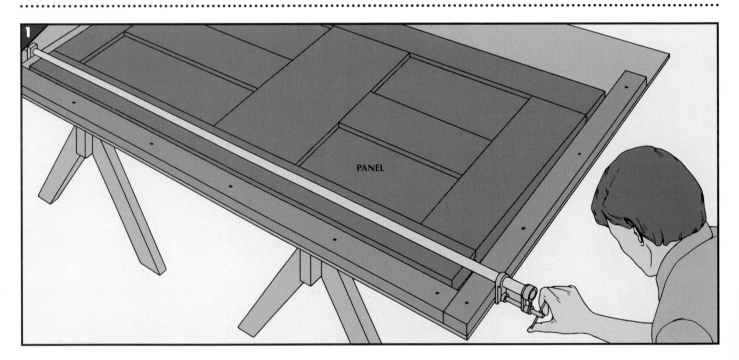

1. Squaring the door.

◆ Prepare a work surface by fastening two 2-by-4s at right angles along two edges of a sheet of plywood.
◆ Remove the door from its hinges and lay it on the work surface.
◆ Carefully spread open the loosest joints, and clean away old glue with a putty knife. Apply wood glue to the inner surfaces, taking care not to spread glue into a joint between a panel and the surrounding wood. The panels must be free to move in their slots, or they will crack as the door swells and shrinks in different seasons.
◆ Before the glue dries, square the door by forcing it into the right angle formed by the 2-by-4s *(above)*—a bar clamp helps if the joints are stiff.
◆ Once the door is square, release the clamp; use it and two others to clamp the door across the width.
◆ Wipe away excess glue with a moist cloth and let the glue dry for 24 hours.

2. Reinforcing a weakened joint.

◆ Mark positions for two dowel holes in the center of the edge of the door and aligned with the joint.

◆ Clamp a drill guide onto the stile at one of the marks and bore a $\frac{1}{2}$-inch hole through the stile and at least 2 inches into the rail, using a drill extension if necessary. Drill the second hole in the same way *(below, left)*.

◆ For a painted door, cut $\frac{1}{2}$-inch fluted wood dowels that are slightly longer than the depth of the holes. For a stained door, cut the dowels $\frac{1}{8}$ inch shorter than the depth of the holes.

◆ Apply glue to both the insides of the holes and the dowels, and then tap the dowels into place *(below, right)*.

◆ Sand the dowels flush before painting the door, or fill the holes with wood putty matching the color of the door.

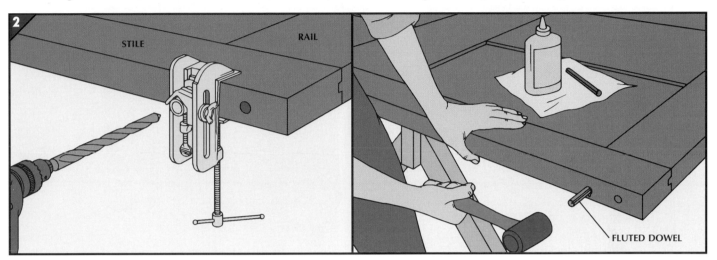

STILE   RAIL   FLUTED DOWEL

A PRIMER ON POCKET DOORS

Diagnosing problems.

Typical pocket doors ride on grooved metal wheels along a track on the floor or overhead. Inside the wall, the doors fit into pockets framed by narrow studs. The top of the door fits between stop moldings *(inset, top);* in some, wood pegs fit in a grooved track to hold the door in line. Double pocket doors have a center stop screwed to the edges of the jamb *(inset, bottom)* to keep doors from sliding past the middle of the opening.

Over time, bits of plaster may pile up in the pockets and can be swept or vacuumed out. A floor track within the opening may be dented or crushed and can be bent back into shape with pliers. Fixing other problems requires removing the doors. For instance, the studs in the pockets sometimes warp and bind the door, or the rollers at the bottom of the door may break. Matching rollers are no longer manufactured, but you may find replacements in secondhand shops, or you can improvise new sets from large window pulleys *(page 65)*.

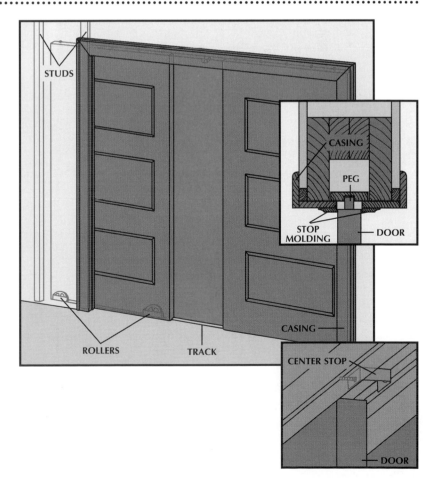

STUDS   CASING   PEG   STOP MOLDING   DOOR   ROLLERS   TRACK   CASING   CENTER STOP   DOOR

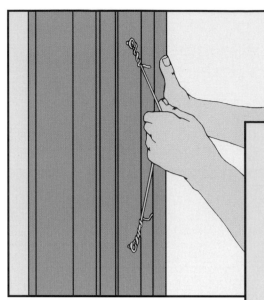

Retrieving a jammed door.

◆ Fasten metal screw eyes into the edge of the door, about 4 feet above the floor and a foot apart.
◆ Run a loop of heavy wire between them, and use the wire as a handle to drag the door out of its pocket.

Removing a door from its frame.

◆ For a double door, unscrew the center stop and slide the door to the middle of the opening, then pry off the stop molding on one side of the top jamb. For a single door, pry off the stop molding on one side of the top jamb, and remove the casing, jamb, and stop on that side as well *(page 63)*.
◆ With a helper, lift the door off its bottom track and gradually slide the bottom of the door sideways until the top of the door is free.

CURING POCKET DOORS THAT BIND

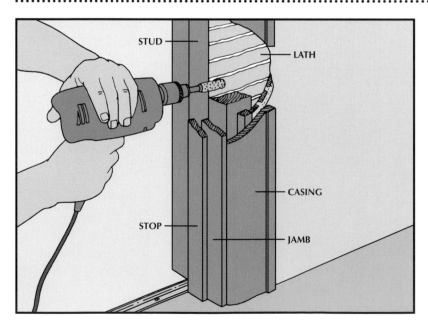

STUD
LATH
CASING
STOP
JAMB

Shaving a warped stud.

◆ If you have not already done so to dismount the door, pry off the casing, jamb, and stop on one side of the door.
◆ Probe inside the pocket with a piece of scrap wood as wide as the door, and note where the scrap binds.
◆ Wearing goggles and working from the middle of the stud toward the top and bottom, shave away about $\frac{1}{8}$ inch of wood with an electric drill fitted with a drum-rasp attachment; move the drill slowly and apply a light, steady pressure.

If studs at the back of the pocket are warped, break through the plaster and lath between studs to get at them, then adapt the procedure shown on pages 46 to 48 to patch the hole.

Improvising new rollers.

◆ Unscrew the old roller assembly and remove it from the deep mortise in the bottom of the door.

◆ Sand or plane a block of wood to slip into the mortise.

◆ Trim the block long enough to reach the bottom of the mortise and align with the shallow faceplate mortises at each side, and wide enough to fit snugly between two large window pulleys set within the mortise *(inset)*.

◆ Cover the faces and an end of the block with glue, tap it into the center of the deep mortise, and fasten it with $1\frac{1}{4}$-inch finishing nails *(right)*.

◆ Let the glue dry for 24 hours, then fasten window pulleys to the door bottom on each side of the block, using $1\frac{1}{2}$-inch-long No. 6 wood screws.

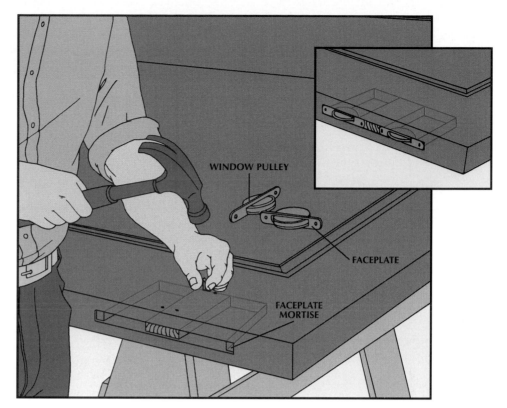

WINDOW PULLEY

FACEPLATE

FACEPLATE MORTISE

Fixing doors suspended from above.

Some pocket doors hang from overhead rollers that you can adjust if the door begins to scrape the floor. To do so, first move the door to the center of the opening. Then tap shims beneath it to lift it $\frac{1}{4}$ inch from the floor, and use a screwdriver or a nutdriver to tighten the adjustment screws on the rollers at each end of the door. If the adjustment screws are not visible at the ends—or if the door has a third roller between the outer ones—remove one of the top casings to expose the screws.

Newer, hollow-core doors are best removed for adjustment. This is a simple matter of lifting door and trolley off the overhead track. With the door dismounted, turn the hexagonal adjustment bolt to lower the wheel $\frac{1}{4}$ inch *(inset)*.

OVERHEAD TRACK

TOP CASING

ADJUSTMENT SCREW

DOOR

ADJUSTMENT BOLT

Making Do with Old Utilities

3

Heating, wiring, and plumbing do not last forever, but there are many steps you can take to maintain the utility systems in an older house. Fireplaces and radiators benefit from inspection and servicing, and leaks in the plumbing can be repaired. With care, even a decades-old electrical system can safely supply power, though added circuits may be needed to accommodate the multitude of modern appliances.

Safe and Efficient Fireplaces   68

Repairing the Chimney Top
Installing a Glass Screen

Reviving Old Wiring   73

Matching the Wires and the Fuses
Working with Armored Cable
Insulation and Switches

Living with a Vintage Heating System   77

Draining the System
Stopping a Radiator-Valve Leak
Servicing an Old-Style Expansion Tank
Balancing a Hot-Air System
Adding an Electric Baseboard Heater

Coping with Antique Plumbing   82

A Patch for a Water Line
Repairing Steel Pipe with Plastic or Copper
A Sleeve for a Drainpipe
Resealing a Drainpipe Joint
Replacing a Section of Cast-Iron Pipe

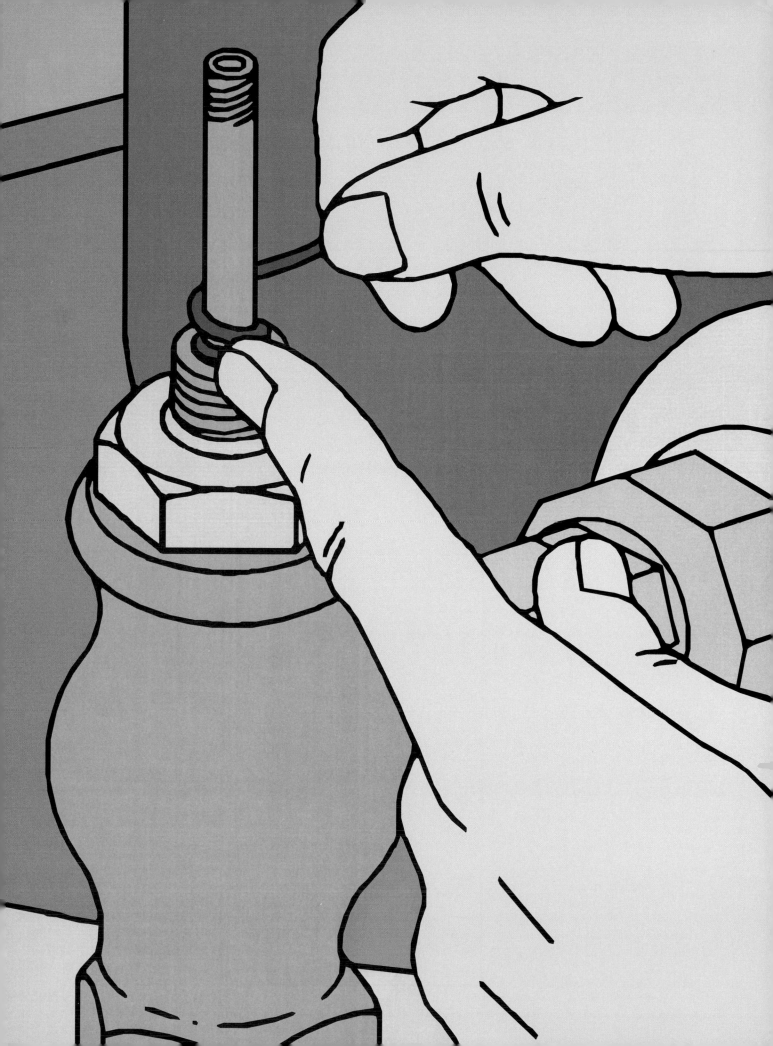

Safe and Efficient Fireplaces

Fireplaces can be among the most attractive features of an old house, but their safety should not be taken for granted. Before using an old fireplace for the first time, check all its crucial parts *(below)*. Particularly important is the flue liner—a duct, normally of terra cotta, that serves as a protective seal for the chimney's interior, preventing leakage of the rising smoke and acting as a heat insulator. You can check for leaks in this lining by the method described at the bottom of the opposite page. If your chimney was built without a liner, or if the liner has misaligned tiles or other structural flaws, ask a chimney sweep for a safety evaluation. It may be necessary to have a liner installed or replaced—a major job.

Cleaning the Chimney: Make sure the flue is clean, and keep it that way: A buildup of soot and creosote in the flue could ignite and cause an intense fire within the chimney, spewing out flame and debris above and below. You can do routine cleaning with flexible rods and a properly fitted brush *(page 70)*, but if the deposits are thick, the services of a chimney sweep may be required.

Exterior Fixes: Check the chimney at its top for signs of deterioration or other problems. If the flashing is faulty and admitting rainwater, you may be able to seal it with roofing cement. Another trouble-prone area is the chimney crown, the mortar pyramid that sits atop the chimney; it can crack and allow water to leak in around the flue's edges. A cracked crown should be patched or rebuilt *(page 70)*.

You may also want to install a rain cap *(page 71)*. This simple addition will provide protection against puddles in the fireplace, keep out warmth-seeking animals, and prevent downdrafts into living spaces.

Fixing a Faulty Draft: If your fireplace smokes chronically, you can improve the draft by reducing the size of the fireplace opening. The interior dimensions of the flue should be roughly one-tenth the area of the fireplace. The easiest way to reduce the opening is to install a glass fire screen *(pages 71-72)*.

 TOOLS

Droplight
Flashlight
Flexible rods and
  brush attachment
Hand-held brush
Vacuum with high
  efficiency partic-
  ulate air (HEPA)
  filter
Ball-peen hammer
Cold chisel
Trowel

 **MATERIALS**

Refractory mortar
Plywood board
Wrap-on fiberglass
  insulation (3")
Silicone adhesive
Duct tape
Fiberglass patch
Sand mortar mix
Stainless-steel rain
  cap with
  setscrews
Glass screen set

 SAFETY TIPS

When cleaning the flue, wear goggles to protect against dust; add a respirator when working from below. Wear gloves and goggles to protect hands and eyes when chipping mortar.

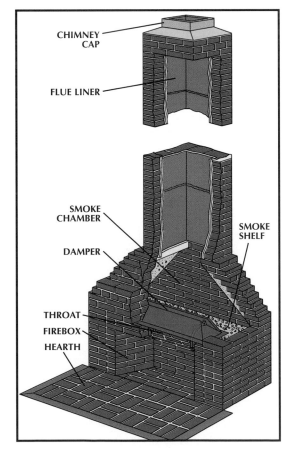

CHIMNEY CAP
FLUE LINER
SMOKE CHAMBER
SMOKE SHELF
DAMPER
THROAT
FIREBOX
HEARTH

Inspecting a flue and fireplace.

◆ Working from the roof, lower a droplight into the flue liner. If soot and creosote obscure its surface, remove enough of these deposits to allow inspection.

◆ Examine the flue liner for cracks, misaligned tiles, and missing mortar in the joints between tiles.

◆ Make sure the chimney cap is solid and uncracked.

◆ Inside the house, check the joint between the firebox floor and the hearth. Loose or crumbling mortar in this area can be repaired with refractory mortar.

◆ Make sure that the damper works and that the smoke shelf is free of debris. Examine the smoke chamber, the throat, and the bottom of the flue liner; repoint any bad joints *(page 123)*.

Whenever you work on the top of a roof, exercise great care. In general, if your roof slopes less than 4 inches in 12, you can move about on it in safety by observing common-sense precautions and wearing rubber-soled shoes. On steep-sloped asphalt roofs, metal supports called roof brackets *(photograph)*, along with a board, offer a platform for a worker and up to 40 pounds of materials for every 4 feet of space *(below)*. The brackets are secured to the sheathing under the shingles with $3\frac{1}{2}$-inch nails driven to within $\frac{1}{4}$ inch of the surface.

Although the slope of the roof is the main factor in determining whether you need to rent or buy special equipment, your personal tolerance for heights is also important: If you feel uncomfortable on a roof regardless of slope, consider hiring a professional to do the work for you. To protect the roof as well as yourself, never walk on a roof made of tile, slate, or wood.

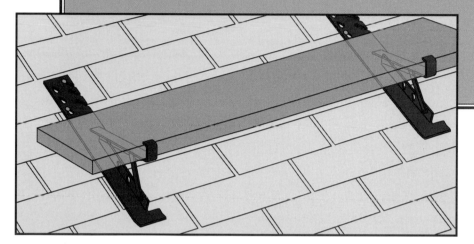

Checking for flue leaks.

◆ Make sure the flue liner and smoke chamber are clean.

◆ Cut a section of plywood board that is 3 inches taller and 6 inches wider than the fireplace opening.

◆ Line the outer perimeter of one side of the board with two layers of 3-inch-wide wrap-on fiberglass insulation, secured with a $1\frac{1}{2}$-inch bead of silicone adhesive.

◆ Prop some wet and dry twisted newspaper on the smoke shelf above the damper *(right)* and light it.

◆ Fit the board against the fireplace, insulation side facing the firebox.

◆ As soon as smoke begins to exit the flue, have a helper on the roof seal the chimney by taping a sturdy plastic bag to it with duct tape.

◆ Check the full length of the chimney for smoke leaks, indoors and out. Where the flue passes behind finished walls, look for leaks under baseboards or around frames of doors and windows; a leak will be easiest to spot if you do this inspection with a flashlight in the dark.

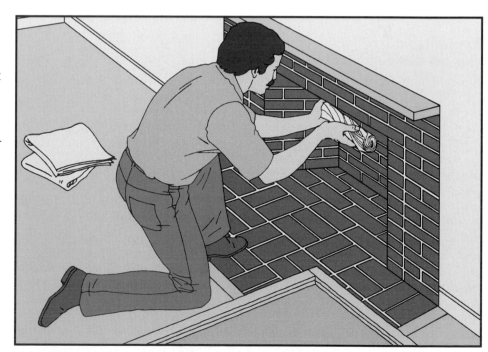

◆ Once the smoke test is done, uncover the chimney top and let the smoke clear for at least 15 minutes before slowly uncovering the fireplace opening.

◆ Clear off the smoke shelf.

Cleaning the flue.

◆ Open the damper and tape two layers of plastic—from sturdy bags—over the fireplace opening.

◆ Remove any screen or cap that is covering the top of the flue.

◆ With flexible rods and a brush attachment sized to fit your flue opening *(left)*, move the brush slowly up and down as you progress down the flue.

◆ Wait an hour for the soot to settle, then unseal the opening and gently remove the debris with a HEPA filter-equipped vacuum. (Soot can ruin a household vacuum.)

◆ With a brush, sweep debris from the smoke shelf into a paper bag held at the fireplace throat.

REPAIRING THE CHIMNEY TOP

Renewing the chimney crown.

◆ If the crown mortar has just a small crack or two, fiberglass patches will be a sufficient seal *(pages 97-98)*.

◆ If the crown is mostly solid but has crumbled in a few places, remove any loose portions, fill the gaps, and cover with new mortar.

◆ For more serious deterioration, chip off the crown with a ball-peen hammer and a cold chisel *(right)*. To avoid damaging the chimney, never direct the chisel toward the bricks.

◆ Brush away the debris and dust, and dampen the area.

◆ Trowel sand mortar on to form a sloping crown that extends from the edge of the brick to about halfway up the side of the top flue liner.

◆ Place the edge of a piece of cardboard—to serve as a spacer—between the mortar and the top of the flue liner, which should extend no more than 4 inches above the top of the crown.

◆ Cover the area with a large plastic bag secured to the side of the chimney with duct tape.

◆ Let the mortar dry for several days, then remove the plastic and the cardboard spacer. Fill the gap left by the spacer with silicone adhesive.

Adding a rain cap.

◆ At a hardware or hearth-products store, buy a stainless-steel rain cap to fit around the perimeter of the flue top.

◆ With a screwdriver, secure the cap to the top of the flue with the setscrews provided with the unit *(left)*.

FLUE   SETSCREWS

INSTALLING A GLASS SCREEN

1. Positioning the frame.

◆ The frame for a glass screen may come with the doors attached; remove them according to the manufacturer's instructions.

◆ Attach fireproof insulation and the mounting-bracket and lintel-clamp assemblies to the back of the screen frame. (The insulation will keep air from flowing in from the sides of the frame.)

◆ Place the frame for the screen over the fireplace opening *(right)*.

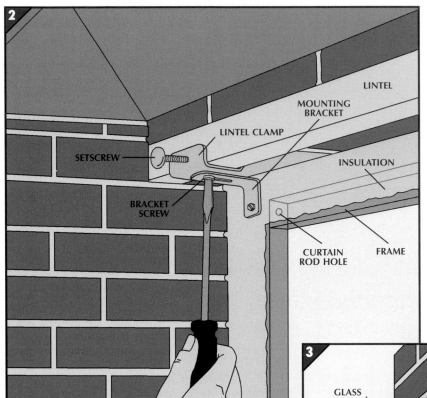

2. Fastening the clamps.

◆ Squatting or lying inside the fireplace, fit each lintel clamp over the lintel and tighten the clamp's setscrew.

◆ Holding the frame firmly against the fireplace opening so that the insulation forms a good seal, tighten the bracket screw that joins the mounting bracket to the lintel clamp *(left)*.

3. Fitting the mesh curtain and doors.

Methods of securing screens—either curtain or rigid types—and glass doors vary. For the unit shown at right, first slip the rod and curtain through the prefabricated holes at the top of the frame. Then slip the two door pins on the side of one door into the pin holes on the side of the frame. Fit on the other door in the same way.

⚠ **CAUTION** *Doors should never be closed when a fire is burning. The glass is not designed to withstand high temperatures.*

Reviving Old Wiring

Old wiring that cannot keep up with a modern array of electrical equipment should be upgraded or replaced as soon as possible. However, if you take the steps described here and on the following pages, the wiring can provide safe, useful service until you are ready to improve it. (An exception is knob-and-tube wiring, illustrated on page 21. It must be replaced immediately.)

Checking the Wires: Whether or not you inspected the wiring before buying the house *(pages 20-21)*, a more detailed examination is in order once you move in. Look over any surface-mounted wiring, which may be installed in metal raceways or tubular conduit or behind flat wood moldings. As long as the insulation around the wires is sound, such wiring is safe. Wood moldings, however, provide little protection and should be replaced.

Some old wiring consists of armored cable, with a flexible metal jacket enclosing separately insulated wires. Examine the wires inside outlets and junction boxes; if the insulation is crumbling, have an electrician conduct a megohm test, which will determine whether electrical leakage is occurring and the circuit must be rewired. In some cases, you may be able to repair bad insulation *(page 76)*.

Checking the Fuses: Next, find the capacity of each circuit by measuring the thickness of the wire *(page 74)*. If the fuse or breaker for that circuit has too high a rating, replace it. This will prevent excessive current in the circuit, which could cause the wire to heat and become a fire hazard.

In a house where fuses blow often, map the circuits by removing fuses or turning off breakers one at a time and observing which outlets and fixtures are affected. Add the wattage of the devices connected to a circuit and divide by 120 to estimate amperes. Then compare these figures with the capacity of the circuits; redistribute loads from heavily used circuits to lightly used ones.

New Switches and Receptacles: Inspect all switches and receptacles. Replace any that spark or get warm as well as receptacles that no longer hold a plug tightly and switches that are hard to operate *(pages 75-76)*.

Armored cable, conduit, or raceway systems are likely to be grounded, providing a continuous path for stray current back to the service panel. If this is the case, you can replace two-slot outlets with safer, grounded three-slot units *(page 75);* some codes require such units whenever you replace a two-slot outlet in an armored cable system. Secure loose armored cable as shown on page 75.

Code Requirements: Local codes vary from community to community. Check with officials to determine if any special requirements apply to the work you plan to do.

TOOLS

Screwdrivers
Voltage tester
Receptacle analyzer

Wire gauge
Heat gun or hair dryer
Wire cutters
Electrical pliers

MATERIALS

Tamperproof adapters
Fuses
Three-slot receptacles

Shrink tubing rated for 300 volts
Ground jumper wires
Light switches

ESSENTIAL SAFEGUARDS

Electric shock is always dangerous and can be fatal. Before working on any electrical box—whether for a switch, receptacle, or light fixture—remove the fuse, or switch off the circuit breaker for that circuit. To make sure you have cut off the correct circuit, use a voltage tester *(photograph)* to check that no current is flowing: Touch the probes of the voltage tester to every combination of wires, terminals, and parts of the box. If the bulb glows, current is still reaching the box; try a different fuse or breaker. If you cannot find the correct one, call an electrician. Once the power is off, label the service panel with a notice so that no one will restore power.

Work on a dry floor, or stand on plywood, and avoid touching plumbing or gas pipes. Afterward, check your finished work with the power on. The voltage tester should glow when one of the leads is touched to an unswitched black wire and the other is touched to a white or bare wire or a part of the metal box. It should not glow on any combination of parts that does not include a black or red wire.

MATCHING THE WIRES AND THE FUSES

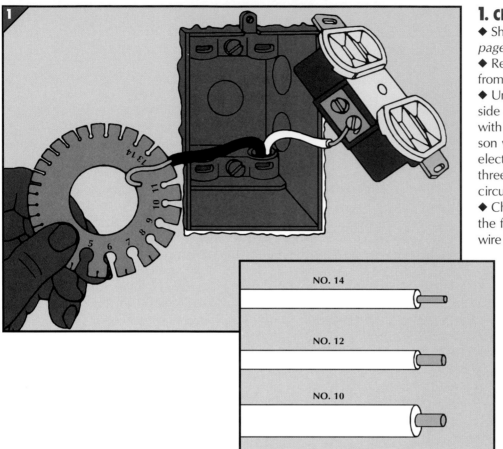

1. Checking the wire size.
◆ Shut off the power to a circuit (box, page 73).
◆ Remove an outlet on that circuit from its box in the wall.
◆ Unscrew one of the wires at the side of the outlet. Measure the wire with a wire gauge (left) or by comparison with short sample lengths from an electrical-parts supplier. Profiles of the three most common gauges of house-circuit wire are shown in the inset.
◆ Check the circuit's wire size against the fuse or breaker. A circuit of No. 14 wire requires a 15-ampere fuse, No. 12 wire a 20-ampere fuse, No. 10 wire a 30-ampere fuse.
◆ Examine each circuit in the same way.

NO. 14

NO. 12

NO. 10

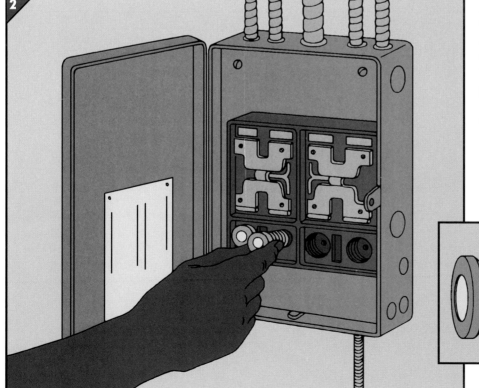

2. Installing tamperproof fuses.
◆ Thread a tamperproof adapter onto a Type S fuse of the size required for each circuit (inset); in Canada, use a Type D fuse. The adapter makes it impossible to use a fuse of the wrong rating in the future.
◆ Screw the fuse-and-adapter assembly into the fuse socket for that circuit (left).

WORKING WITH ARMORED CABLE

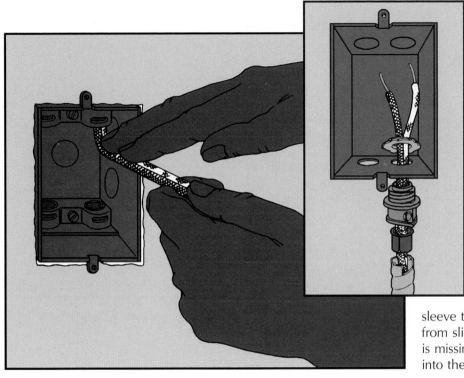

Tightening up on armored cable.
If the metal jacket of armored cable comes free of the clamp that holds it to the box, the ground contact can be lost. Restore the connection as follows:
◆ With the power turned off, loosen the box clamp.
◆ Pull the cable back into the box, guiding it with both hands *(left)*.
◆ Tighten the clamp.

If the clamp is located outside of the box *(inset)*, you must make a hole in the wall to reach it; be sure the nut that holds the external clamp from inside the box is tight. At the end of each cable, look for a red insulating sleeve that prevents the cut edge of the metal from slicing into the wire insulation. If the sleeve is missing, try to slip one around the wires and into the cable end.

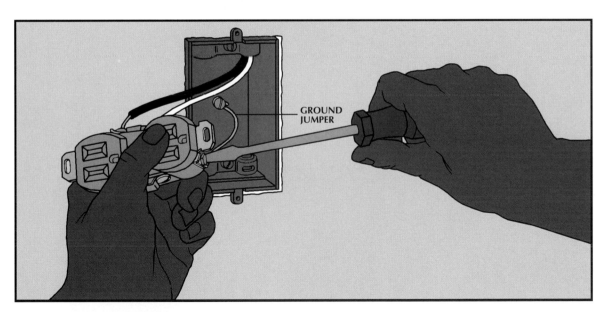

GROUND
JUMPER

Replacing a receptacle.
Install a grounded three-slot receptacle in place of a two-slot unit as follows:
◆ Perform a ground-continuity test *(page 21)* to make sure grounding connections have not become loose. If they have, tighten the cable's connection to the box and test again.
◆ Turn off power to the circuit, remove the cover plate, and pull the old receptacle out of the box.
◆ Unscrew the wires from the old receptacle and then screw them to the new receptacle; the white wire goes to a silver terminal, and

the black wire goes to a brass terminal.
◆ To add the ground connection, screw a ground jumper wire to the box and to the green terminal on the receptacle *(above)*.
◆ Perform another ground-continuity test to verify that the new receptacle is grounded.

Some outlet boxes have a cable from the power source and one leading on to another box. Connect the two white wires of such a pair of cables to the silver terminals of the receptacle and the two black wires to the brass terminals.

INSULATION AND SWITCHES

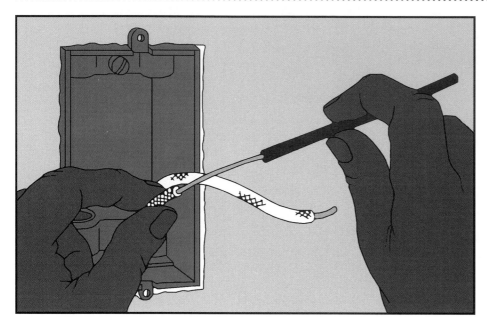

Shielding a wire with tubing.
In most cases, a circuit should be rewired if the insulation of a wire in a box has deteriorated or crumbles when touched. You can simply replace the insulation, however, if the damage does not extend all the way to the point where the wire leaves the box.
◆ With the power off, strip the deteriorated insulation from its wire.
◆ Slip shrink tubing rated at 300 volts or more over the bare wire *(left)*, making sure to extend it over the end of the remaining wire insulation.
◆ Blow hot air on the tubing with a heat gun or hair dryer until the tubing tightens into place.

Replacing a switch.
◆ Shut off power to the old switch, take off the cover plate, and remove the switch from the box *(left)*.
◆ Attach the wires to the terminals of a new switch in the same way they were attached to the old. Take care to orient a toggle switch so that the words ON and OFF are upright.
◆ Replace the cover plate. If you are replacing a push-button switch with a toggle switch, you will need a new plate.

If the old switch has three terminals, it is part of a three-way circuit. Make a note of the wiring connections before removing the switch, and connect the wires in the same way when you replace it.

Living with a Vintage Heating System

Replacement may be the proper choice for some old heating equipment, but if yours is mechanically sound, it could continue to provide adequate heat for years. A thorough inspection by a professional will bring to light any major problems; but you can make minor adjustments, repairs, and additions that will help improve the system's effectiveness.

Hot-Water and Steam Heat: When one or two radiators remain cold while the rest heat up, air may be trapped inside, preventing water or steam from entering. In a hot-water system, bleed radiators or replace malfunctioning bleed valves *(below)*. Use the same procedure to replace a faulty air vent in a steam system.

If a shutoff valve on a radiator leaks, first try tightening the packing nut a quarter-turn; if the valve still leaks, repack it *(page 79)*. Try tightening other screw-together parts of a leaky valve. If necessary, replace the valve *(page 79)*. In a hot-water system this requires draining the system through the boiler *(page 78)*, a procedure that is necessary for some other repairs—replacing deteriorated steel pipe with copper *(pages 82-84)*, for example—but not as a point of periodic maintenance.

From time to time, however, you may have to drain the expansion tank. Usually located near the boiler, it provides a temporary reservoir for boiler water, which expands when heated. If the temperature-pressure gauge on the boiler indicates 30 pounds per square inch (psi) or more—or if the safety valve spouts water—drain the tank if it is the old, diaphragmless type *(pages 79-80)*. Recharge a newer tank to a pressure of about 20 psi with a bicycle pump attached to the air valve.

Hot-Air Heat: If some rooms are warm while others are cold, the dampers in the ducts may need adjusting *(page 80)*; also check that the dampers behind registers are open. You may want to replace old-fashioned registers with modern, adjustable deflector grilles.

An Auxiliary Heater: If the furnace, radiators, and registers are working properly and you still have a cold room, the problem is solved most easily with a self-contained electric baseboard heating unit *(pages 80-81)*. Installing a 20-amp branch circuit from the service panel for a 240-volt heater is the best solution; 120-volt units designed for direct connection to house wiring are uncommon, and a plug-in model can easily overload the circuit that serves it *(pages 20-21 and 73-74)*. Have an electrician make the connections at the service panel if you are unsure about doing the job safely yourself.

 TOOLS

Screwdriver	Two pipe wrenches	Twist bit ($\frac{1}{8}$")
Small adjustable wrench	Electronic stud finder	Fish tape
	Electric drill	Cable ripper
	Spade bit ($\frac{3}{4}$")	Wire stripper

 **MATERIALS**

Absorbent rags	Graphite packing cord	2-wire grounded cable (No. 12)
Plumbing-sealant tape	Garden hose	Wood screws (1")
Wood shims	240-volt electric baseboard heating unit	Wire caps
		Single-pole thermostat

Bleeding a hot-water radiator.

Have an absorbent rag handy; when all of the air is vented, hot water will begin to escape from the bleed valve.

On manual valves with a knob, turn the knob 180 degrees counterclockwise; on those without a knob, use a screwdriver *(inset)* or radiator-venting key. Automatic bleed valves normally bleed themselves, but if one is clogged, press the stem in the center of the valve to bleed it as you would a car tire. Close any of these valves as soon as water escapes in a steady stream.

If a valve drips constantly or will not bleed at all, replace it. To do so, close the radiator shutoff valve and use a wrench to unscrew the bleed valve. Wrap the threads of the new valve with plumbing-sealant tape and screw it in place.

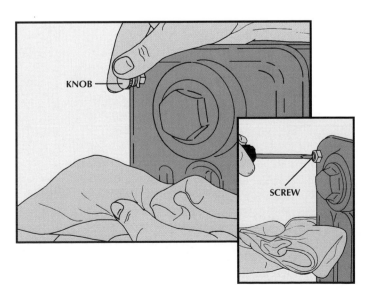

KNOB

SCREW

Quieting a Steam System

Houses with steam heat are sometimes plagued by loud knocking noises when the furnace is running. The cause is steam trying to rise through water that has collected in low spots in the system as a result of pipes and radiators sagging or settling over the years. To banish the racket, shim radiators so that water can run out of the pipe in one end *(right)*. Also check for broken pipe-support straps *(inset)*; repair them, raising the pipe so that it slopes toward the boiler.

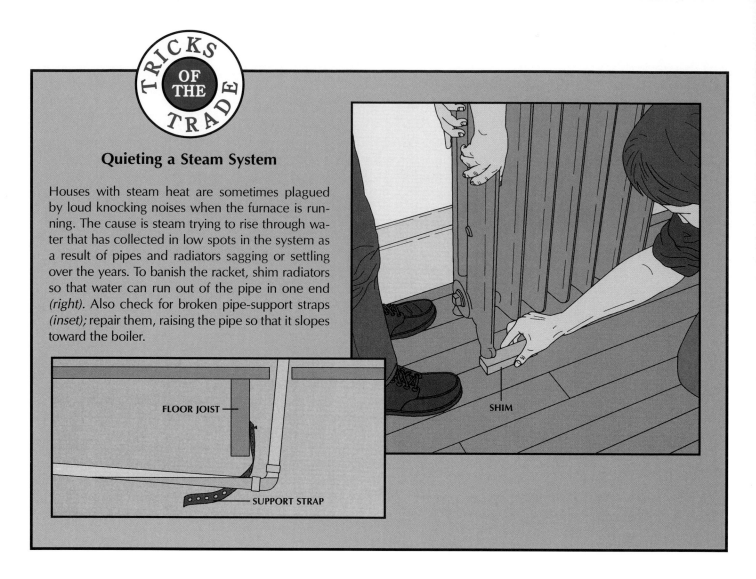

FLOOR JOIST

SUPPORT STRAP

SHIM

DRAINING THE SYSTEM

Emptying and refilling the boiler.

◆ Turn off power to the boiler at the service panel and master switch.

◆ Check the temperature-pressure gauge on the boiler; when the temperature falls below 100°F, close the shutoff valve.

◆ Attach a hose to the boiler drain cock and run the hose to a floor drain, then open the drain cock and all the radiator bleed valves.

◆ When water no longer flows, empty the expansion tank if it is equipped with a drain *(page 79)*.

◆ To refill the system, close the radiator bleed valves and the boiler drain cock. Open the main shutoff valve and the expansion tank shutoff valve.

◆ Watch the temperature-pressure gauge: When the pressure reaches 5 psi, bleed every radiator in the house, starting on the ground floor *(page 77)*.

◆ After the boiler pressure stabilizes (on most systems, at 15 to 20 psi), restore power to the boiler.

◆ Allow heated water to circulate until the radiators are warm, then bleed each radiator again.

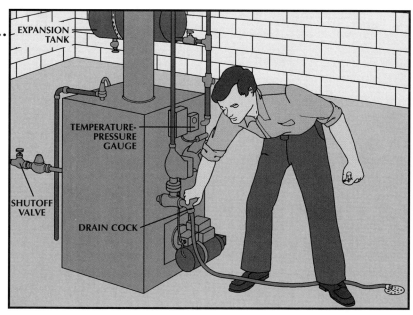

EXPANSION TANK

TEMPERATURE-PRESSURE GAUGE

SHUTOFF VALVE

DRAIN COCK

⚠ *Never turn on the power to the system before refilling it.*
CAUTION

STOPPING A RADIATOR-VALVE LEAK

1. Removing the handle and packing nut.

◆ Close the shutoff valve and place rags around it; when you loosen the packing nut, the leaking may increase.

◆ Remove the screw in the center of the handle *(right)*, and pull the handle off the stem.

◆ Apply one wrench to the valve body to hold it steady and use another to unscrew the packing nut from the stem.

◆ Scrape out any old packing from the nut and around the stem.

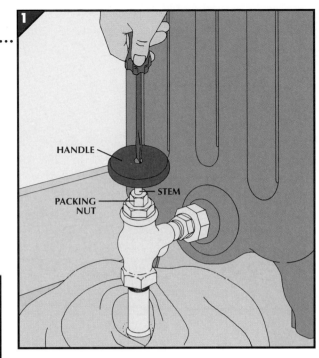

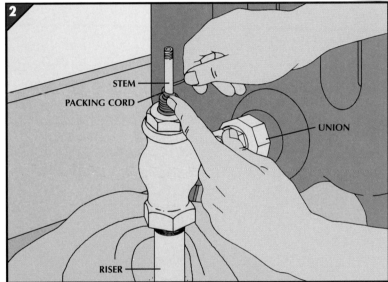

2. Packing the stem.

◆ Wrap two or three turns of graphite packing cord clockwise around the bottom of the stem *(left)*.

◆ Replace the packing nut, being careful not to overtighten it, then open the valve.

If the valve still leaks, replace it: Drain the system *(page 78)* and disconnect the valve from the radiator at the union. Grasp the body of the valve and the riser with pipe wrenches and unscrew the valve. Wrap plumbing-sealant tape around exposed threads before screwing the new valve into place.

SERVICING AN OLD-STYLE EXPANSION TANK

1. Draining the tank.

◆ Turn off power at the service panel and master switch and allow the boiler to cool, then close the expansion tank shutoff valve *(right)*.

◆ Run a garden hose from the drain cock on the bottom of the expansion tank to a floor drain or laundry sink, then open the drain cock.

◆ Use a wrench to open the air-release valve on the side of the tank *(inset)*. If the tank has no air-release valve, loosen the union between the tank and the boiler until you hear a hissing sound. Keep a rag handy; the union will leak a little.

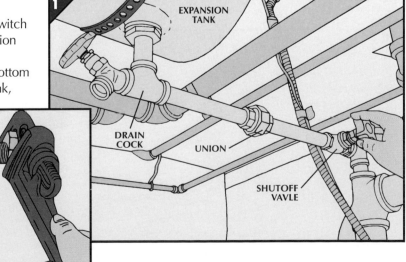

79

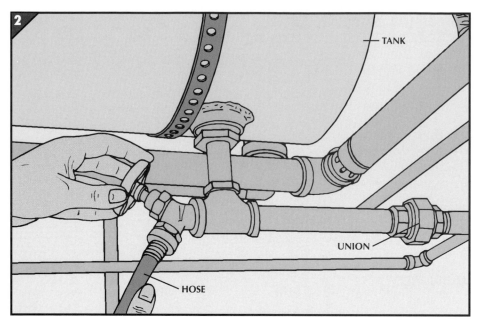

TANK

UNION

HOSE

2. Refilling the tank.
◆ When the tank has drained completely, close the drain cock *(left)*.
◆ Tighten the air-release valve or the union, and partially open the tank's shutoff valve. You will hear water slowly entering the tank; after the sound stops, open the valve completely.
◆ When the temperature-pressure gauge on the boiler reads about 15 psi, restore power to the boiler.
◆ Allow the radiators to become warm, then bleed all of them *(page 77)*. After several hours, bleed them again.

BALANCING A HOT-AIR SYSTEM

Adjusting the dampers.
◆ Locate the damper handles on ducts where they branch off a main duct or where they exit the furnace plenum.
◆ Adjust a damper by turning the handle. When it is parallel to the duct *(right)*, the damper is fully open. Turn the handle perpendicular to the duct to close the damper all the way.
◆ Run the system for a few hours, then check temperatures in rooms and readjust dampers as needed.

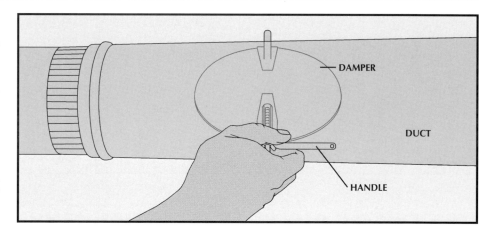

DAMPER

DUCT

HANDLE

ADDING AN ELECTRIC BASEBOARD HEATER

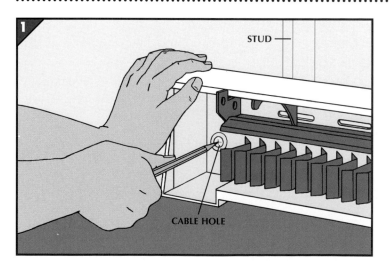

STUD

CABLE HOLE

1. Positioning the heater.
◆ Remove a section of baseboard and use a stud finder to locate and mark studs behind the wall.
◆ Remove the access panels from both ends of the heater, and the metal tab, or knockout, for the electrical cable.
◆ Place the heater against the wall with its mounting holes aligned with the studs, and mark the location of the hole for the electrical cable.

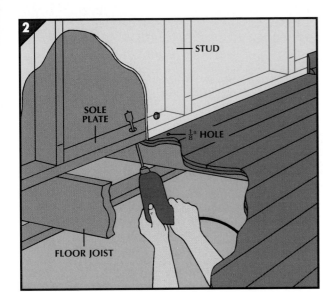

2. Drilling for the cable.

◆ Set the heater aside, and with a $\frac{3}{4}$-inch spade bit, drill a hole in the wall at the mark.
◆ Directly beneath the hole, drill a $\frac{1}{8}$-inch hole through the floor and insert a thin wire.
◆ Go to the basement and locate the wire, then drill a $\frac{3}{4}$-inch hole up through the sole plate, opposite the wire.

3. Routing the cable.

◆ Push the end of a fish tape through the hole in the wall, and have a helper push another fish tape up through the hole in the sole plate. Hook them together behind the wall.
◆ From the basement, pull the fish tapes through the sole plate until the end of the upper one is exposed, then unhook the tapes.
◆ With a cable ripper, strip 8 inches of sheathing from one end of a length of No. 12 two-conductor electrical cable and remove about $\frac{1}{2}$ inch of insulation from the wires.
◆ Wrap the wires around the hook of the fish tape and secure them with tape.
◆ Withdraw the fish tape from the hole as your helper feeds cable through the sole plate. Pull 2 or 3 feet of cable through the hole, then detach the wires from the fish tape.

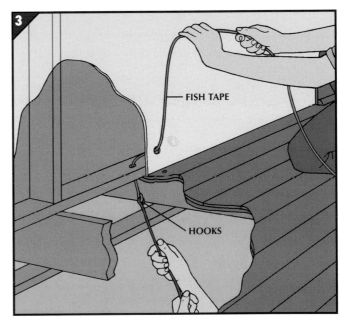

4. Connecting the wires.

◆ Feed the cable through the knockout hole in the heater and secure it with a cable clamp, then screw the heater to the wall studs with 1-inch wood screws.
◆ Join the cable's black wire to one of the black heater wires.
◆ Recode the white wire of the cable with black tape and connect it to the other black heater wire.
◆ Attach the ground wire of the cable to the ground screw of the heater.
◆ Mount a single-pole thermostat in the access panel at the opposite end of the heater, then join the heater wires to the thermostat wires (inset).

Run the cable to the service panel, then have an electrician make the connection.

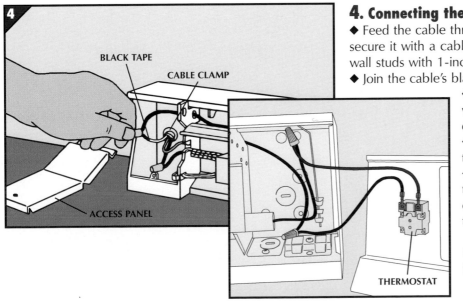

Water-supply pipes and drainpipes in some old houses are obsolete or well on their way to becoming so. But unless your plans call for a major renovation of the house, you can extend the life of the plumbing by patching it or replacing it piece by piece.

In most cases, modern parts can be used to repair old fixtures such as bathtubs, sinks, toilets, and lavatories. A more serious problem in old plumbing systems is the deterioration of pipes.

Old Pipe Materials: As explained on page 22, galvanized-steel supply pipes eventually succumb to rust and corrosion. Cast iron, which is the material most commonly used in old drainpipes, has proved to be more durable, but over the years it also can rust.

You may also find lead pipe. Since lead is toxic, replace supply pipes of this material as soon as is practical; drainpipes can be repaired.

Stopping Leaks: Though steel supply piping eventually must be replaced, leaks can be patched temporarily *(below)*. Drainpipe leaks need a larger patch *(page 85);* those around joints sometimes can be cured by tamping down the lead *(page 85)* or repacking the joint *(page 86)*.

Replacing Pipes: When pipe has deteriorated so much that simple patches are impractical, you will have to cut out and replace the bad sections. Substitute pipes that are made of copper or plastic—chlorinated polyvinyl chloride (CPVC)—for steel supply pipes.

To splice copper or CPVC to steel, you need one of the transition fittings shown at right. Before replacing steel pipe, have an electri-cian check to see if the plumbing is part of your home's electrical grounding system, and if necessary, have a grounding jumper installed to bridge the new section of pipe.

Replace cast-iron drainpipes with sections of the same material or of another plastic called polyvinyl chloride (PVC). Splice together the sections with flexible hubless fittings *(page 87)*. Replace lead drainpipes the same way.

> ⚠️ **CAUTION** *Primer and cement for plastic pipe are toxic and flammable; work in a well-ventilated room, and do not smoke. Solder together copper pipe and fittings at a workbench whenever possible. If you must solder pipes in place, dampen nearby wood before beginning, place a flameproof pad behind the work, and keep a fire extinguisher handy.*

 TOOLS

SUPPLY PIPE REPAIRS

Adjustable wrench
Hacksaw
Two pipe wrenches
Tube cutter
Propane torch
Flameproof pad

DRAINPIPE REPAIRS

Cold chisel
Ball-peen hammer
Yarn iron
Caulking irons
Ratchet pipe cutter
Nutdriver

 MATERIALS

SUPPLY PIPE REPAIRS

Pipe sleeve
CPVC adapters
Dielectric unions
Plumbing-sealant tape
CPVC pipe
CPVC primer and cement
Copper pipe
Sandcloth
Flux
Solder

DRAINPIPE REPAIRS

Oakum
Lead wool
Pipe clamp
2 x 4s
Hubless fittings

🪖 **SAFETY TIPS**

Protect your eyes with goggles when cutting pipe above eye level; add heavy-duty work gloves for soldering with a propane torch.

A PATCH FOR A WATER LINE

A pipe sleeve.
To patch a minor leak in a supply pipe, use a pipe sleeve—a metal sleeve with a rubber gasket, available at hardware stores.

◆ Spread apart the flanges and slip the sleeve around the pipe.
◆ Turn the flanges away from the leak and tighten the bolts.

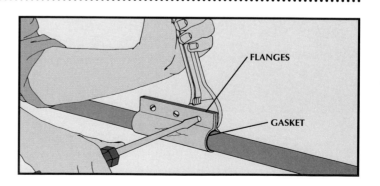

FLANGES

GASKET

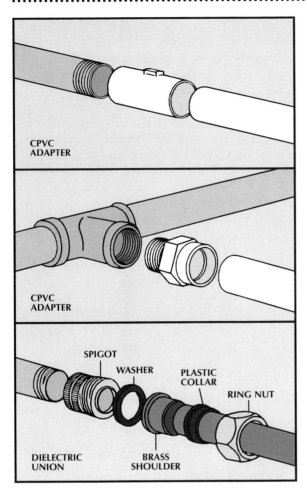

CPVC ADAPTER

CPVC ADAPTER

SPIGOT WASHER PLASTIC COLLAR RING NUT

DIELECTRIC UNION BRASS SHOULDER

Three transition fittings.

Steel-to-plastic supply pipe fittings—called CPVC adapters—come in two types. One has interior threads to screw onto an existing steel pipe *(top)*; the other has exterior threads to screw into a steel fitting *(center)*. The smooth bore at the other end of either fitting is for cementing to plastic pipe.

A steel-to-copper fitting, called a dielectric union *(bottom)*, prevents galvanic corrosion, which can occur between dissimilar metals. It consists of a threaded steel spigot that fits the steel pipe, a brass shoulder for the copper pipe, and a plastic collar and a neoprene washer to separate the two metals. A steel ring nut clamps the union together.

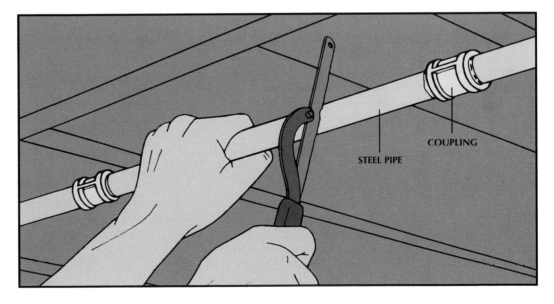

COUPLING

STEEL PIPE

Removing steel pipe.

◆ Cut the pipe with a hacksaw and unscrew the resulting pieces from the nearest couplings using two pipe wrenches.
◆ Reposition the wrenches and remove the couplings, then wrap plumbing-sealant tape around the pipe threads thus exposed.
◆ For plastic replacement pipe, screw CPVC adapters onto the ends of the steel pipe; for copper replacement pipe, screw the steel spigot of a dielectric union onto the threads.

If the nearest steel fitting is a T or an elbow instead of a coupling, leave it in place. Attach plastic pipe to a T or elbow using a CPVC adapter with exterior threads; for copper pipe, screw a short steel nipple—a length of pipe threaded at both ends—into the steel fitting before attaching a dielectric union.

Measure the gap in the steel pipe and cut a piece of replacement pipe to that length, including the depth of the fittings. Cut CPVC with a hacksaw, copper with a tube cutter.

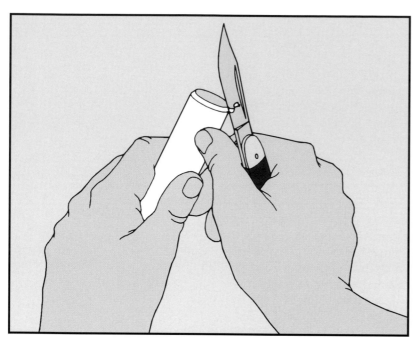

Cementing CPVC and adapters.
◆ Use a pocketknife to bevel the outside edge of the pipe end *(left)*.
◆ Paint CPVC primer around the outside of the pipe end, then coat the inside of an adapter.
◆ Working quickly—CPVC cement hardens within seconds—apply a thick coating of cement to the pipe end, and a thinner one inside the adapter.
◆ Push the pipe into the fitting and twist it a quarter-turn to spread the cement evenly.
◆ Do not run water through the connection for about 2 hours.

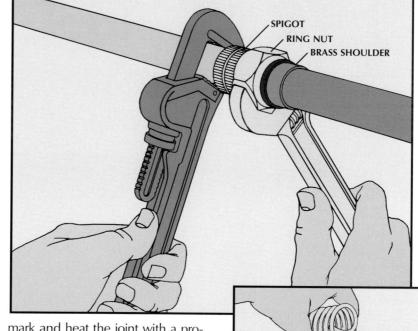

SPIGOT
RING NUT
BRASS SHOULDER

BRASS SHOULDER
PLASTIC COLLAR
RING NUT

Installing a dielectric union.
◆ Deburr the cut end of the copper replacement pipe. Smooth inside edges with the reaming blade on the tube cutter, outside edges with a file.
◆ Temporarily install the copper pipe, using a pipe wrench to hold the steel pipe while you tighten both union ring nuts *(right)*.
◆ Mark the copper pipe at the base of the brass shoulders.
◆ Remove the pipe and extract the neoprene washers from the ring nuts, then slide the ring nuts and plastic collars toward the center of the pipe.
◆ Scour the inside of the brass shoulder with a wire brush and, with plumber's abrasive sandcloth, brighten the outside of the pipe to a distance slightly beyond the marks, but do not touch them; even a fingerprint will weaken the joint.
◆ Apply a thin coat of soldering flux to the cleaned surfaces with a small brush.
◆ Slip the pipe into a shoulder up to the mark and heat the joint with a propane torch.
◆ When the solder melts on contact with the pipe, remove the torch and feed solder into the joint until a bead appears around the rim *(inset)*. Solder the other shoulder and then let the joints cool.
◆ Slide the ring nuts over the sleeves and place the neoprene washers inside, then install the replacement pipe permanently as before.

A SLEEVE FOR A DRAINPIPE

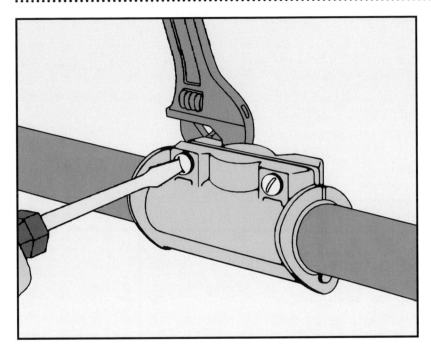

Sealing a minor leak.
Installed in the same way as the supply pipe sleeve *(page 82)*, a heavier sleeve—available at plumbing-supply stores—is used to patch small leaks in drain lines.

RESEALING A DRAINPIPE JOINT

1. Tamping the lead.
◆ With a cold chisel and a ball-peen hammer, gently tap the lead into the joint. Do not use excessive force; hard blows could crack the joint.
◆ Run water through the pipe. If the joint still leaks, move to the next step.

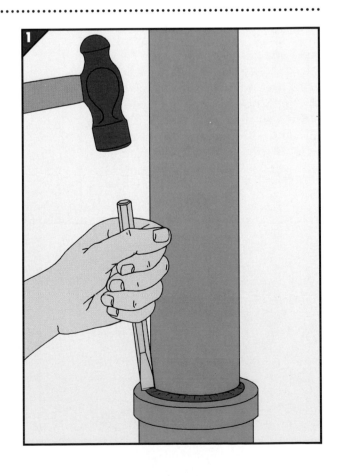

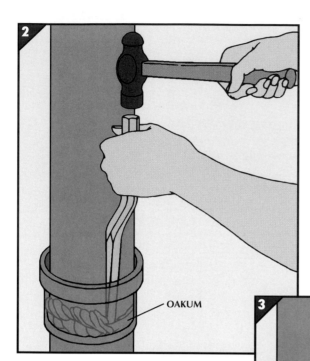

OAKUM

2. Replacing the oakum.

◆ Pry the old lead from around the joint with a thin chisel or a screwdriver. If the lead does not come out easily, heat the joint with a propane torch to soften it.

◆ Next, remove the oakum—the ropelike, oily material that seals the joint under the lead.

◆ Repack the hub with new oakum, pressing it down tightly with a hammer and a yarn iron, which is designed for this purpose and available at plumbing-supply stores.

◆ Leave at least an inch of space between the oakum and the top of the hub.

3. Caulking the joint.

◆ Wrap a length of lead wool (photograph) around the pipe and press it tight against the oakum.

◆ Use two different caulking irons—tools resembling a yarn iron but with beveled tips—to lock the lead wool into the joint. Position an inside caulking iron—its beveled edge faces outward—against the inner pipe and tamp the lead wool down about $\frac{1}{8}$ inch. Next, hold an outside caulking iron (inset)—its beveled edge faces inward—between the outer pipe and the lead wool and tap it with the hammer.

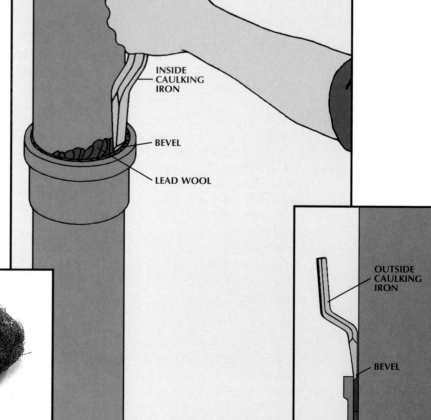

INSIDE CAULKING IRON

BEVEL

LEAD WOOL

OUTSIDE CAULKING IRON

BEVEL

REPLACING A SECTION OF CAST-IRON PIPE

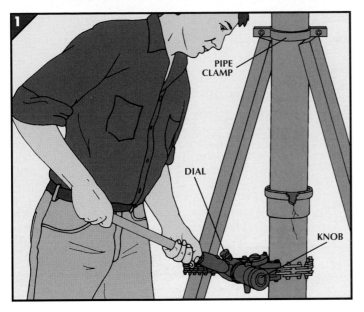

1. Cutting the pipe.

◆ With a pipe clamp and 2-by-4s, brace the pipe above the place where you will cut.
◆ Wrap the chain of a ratchet pipe cutter around the pipe below the damaged section and hook it onto the tool.
◆ Tighten the chain with the knob, turn the dial to CUT, then work the tool up and down until the pipe separates.
◆ Cut through the pipe above the damaged section and pull it out.
◆ Stuff rags or paper towels into the lower pipe to prevent sewer gas from escaping.
◆ Use the pipe cutter to cut a section of new pipe $\frac{1}{4}$ inch shorter than the damaged piece you cut out.

2. Replacing the pipe section.

◆ Slip the neoprene sleeves of two hubless fittings over the ends of the drainpipe and slide the fittings' steel bands, each fitted with two clamps, onto the new section of pipe.
◆ Fold the sleeves back onto themselves *(right)*, then remove the rags or paper towels from the lower pipe.
◆ Push the new section of pipe into place, then unfold the sleeves to cover the joints.

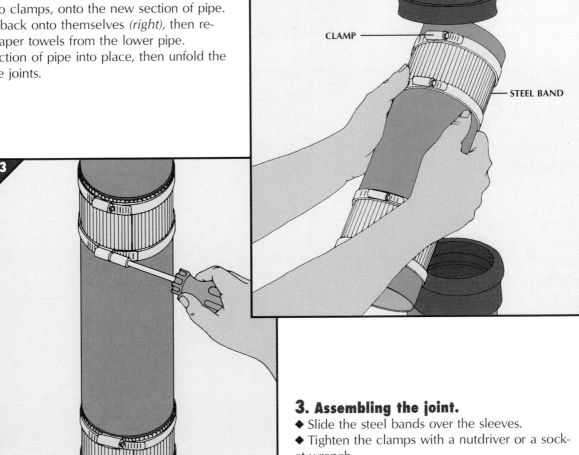

3. Assembling the joint.

◆ Slide the steel bands over the sleeves.
◆ Tighten the clamps with a nutdriver or a socket wrench.
◆ After a week, check the joint and retighten the clamps if necessary.

Maintaining a Sound Structure

4

The structural features of old houses are often superior to those of today. Masonry walls are massive, and wood framing may be thicker and stronger. Yet old houses are just as vulnerable to rot, stress, weather, and termites as any modern dwelling—and may have been subjected to any of these for much longer. Consult this chapter to ward off future damage and to repair existing structural flaws.

Keeping a Roof in Good Condition   90

A Variety of Small Repairs
Removing Slates, Tiles, or Wood Shingles
Installing Replacements
Drip Edges and Gutters
Reinforcing the Roof Frame

Bandaging Surface Cracks   97

Patching a Flat Surface
Special Techniques for Corners and Curves

Shields against Moisture and Dirt   100

Preparing Wood Siding for Paint
Surface Cleaning for Masonry

Patching Holes in Stucco   104

Restoring Outside Walls   106

Sheathing for a Wood Sill
Repairing Rotted Cornices
Replacing Damaged Sections of Siding
Supports for a Masonry Opening

Correcting Floor Sags   112

Bracing a Weak Spot
Leveling a Floor from Below
Lifting a Floor from Outside
Replacing Part of a Sill Plate
Repairs for Joists in a Frame House
Reinforcing Joists in a Masonry House
Splints for Rotted Studs

Remedies for Ailing Foundations   122

Patching and Pointing
Underpinning a Foundation Wall

Reseating protective flashing →

Keeping a Roof in Good Condition

Roof leaks and gutter problems often start small, but they can cause major damage to the house if left uncorrected. Clean out the gutters at least twice a year, and at the same time check for flaws in gutters, roofing, and flashing. Some defects may not be noticed until water enters the house during a storm. In that case, catch the drips in buckets and wait for the rain to end—and the roof to dry—before getting up on the roof to begin repairs.

Patches for the Roofing: The simplest faults to detect and remedy are leaks in the broad expanse of the roof itself. Asphalt shingles may be torn, worn, or curled. Wood shingles can rot, and slates or tiles can crack. In some cases, shingles, slates, or tiles may be missing altogether. Unless the damage is so severe that complete reroofing is required *(page 12)*, confine your repairs to a small area consisting of one or two damaged pieces. Trying to repair a larger expanse can disturb the overall pattern of the roofing and cause more problems than are solved.

Fixing Flaws in the Flashing: Somewhat harder to find and remedy are leaks under flashing—the metal strips that seal joints where roof slopes converge or where the roof meets a wall, chimney, or vent pipe. Examine flashing to see that it is unbroken and that the edges are sealed. If the house has an unfinished attic, you can check for leaks from inside: Look for daylight, and mark any opening by poking a wire through.

Flashing is available in copper, aluminum, zinc, or galvanized steel; when you must replace a section of flashing, match the metal you already have to avoid galvanic corrosion. Roofing cement seals flashing best on most roofs.

Gutter Repairs: After you clean the gutters, spray the roof with a hose and watch the gutters for pooling—a sign of sagging or other misalignment. Also inspect the gutter surfaces; vinyl, aluminum, and copper gutters rarely need maintenance, but rust may develop in steel gutters and rot in wood ones. You can patch small holes *(page 99);* replace large sections that are damaged. Paint steel gutters every few years, and coat wood gutters with a preservative annually.

Strengthening the Roof: Although you should never try to reverse a sag in the roof, you can keep it from getting worse. Two bracing methods are shown on page 96; both are effective but can cause hairline cracks in plaster below. A third way to reinforce a roof is to install sister rafters and joists cut to the same size as the old counterparts and nailed to them.

⚠️ **CAUTION** *Consult page 69 for precautions to take when you work on a roof. To avoid causing further damage, never walk on a slate, tile, or wood-shingle roof.*

 TOOLS

Hammer
Roofer's mop or push broom
Ball-peen hammer
Cold chisel or brick set
Slate ripper
Hacksaw blade
Electric drill
Tin snips
Plumb bob
Mallet
Carpenter's level

 **MATERIALS**

Roofing cement
Galvanized roofing nails ($1\frac{1}{4}$")
Flashing
Fibrous aluminum roof coating
Masonry nails ($\frac{3}{4}$")
Slates
Clay tiles
Wood shingles

Drip edge
Gutter spike
Ferrule
Sheet-metal screws
Lumber (2 x 4, 2 x 6, 4 x 4)
Common nails ($2\frac{1}{2}$")

 SAFETY TIPS

Wear soft-soled, slip-resistant shoes when working on a roof. When you clean gutters, gloves will protect against sharp metal edges and such debris as roofing nails and thorns. Goggles guard your eyes when you are hammering, and a hard hat is advisable in an unfinished attic.

A VARIETY OF SMALL REPAIRS

Mending a torn shingle.
◆ Spread a thin coating of roofing cement under a damaged asphalt shingle.
◆ Press the flaps flat and drive galvanized roofing nails along each side of the tear *(left)*.
◆ Cover the nailheads and the tear with roofing cement.

Patching a crack with metal.
◆ As a temporary measure to stop leaks through a cracked wood shingle or slate, cut a piece of metal flashing that is twice the width of and 3 inches longer than the exposed part of the damaged shingle.
◆ Spread roofing cement on one side of the flashing along what will be the upper edge.

Insert that edge under the broken shingle and the adjacent shingles, with the cemented side down.
◆ Use a wood block and a hammer to tap the flashing in until its upper edge extends under the lower edges of the shingles in the course above *(right)*.
◆ For a more permanent repair, remove and replace the broken piece *(pages 92-94)*.

Coating pitted or pinholed metal.
You can extend the life of a pitted metal roof somewhat by applying fibrous aluminum roof coating with a roofer's mop or a stiff-bristled push broom *(left)*. Work the coating well into all valleys and joints. Most coatings last about a year; since a second layer is not recommended, plan to replace the roof within that time.

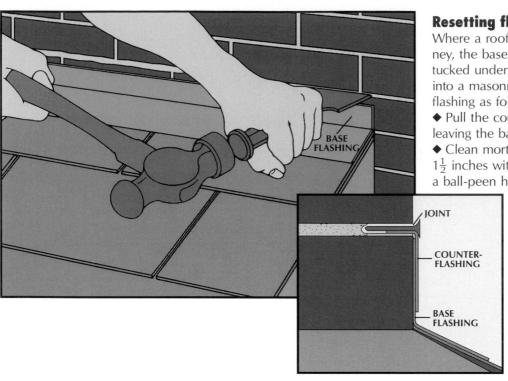

Resetting flashing in a mortar joint.

Where a roof joins a masonry wall or chimney, the base flashing on the roof is generally tucked underneath counterflashing inserted into a masonry joint. Reseat loose counterflashing as follows:

◆ Pull the counterflashing out of the way, leaving the base flashing in place.

◆ Clean mortar out of the joint to a depth of $1\frac{1}{2}$ inches with a cold chisel or brick set and a ball-peen hammer *(left)*.

◆ Refill the joint with roofing cement, push in the lip of the counterflashing, and drive a masonry nail above it near the top of the joint so that it wedges the counterflashing in place without piercing it *(inset)*. For a long section, place a masonry nail every 2 feet.

◆ Seal the metal-to-masonry joint with roofing cement.

REMOVING SLATES, TILES, OR WOOD SHINGLES

Extracting broken remnants.

◆ Slide the arrow-shaped head of a slate ripper *(photograph)*—a special-purpose tool available at roofing-supply stores—under a broken slate, wood shingle, or clay tile. Hook an end notch around a nail. The nails holding tiles are located along the flat section of the tile *(inset)*.

◆ Cut the nail with a sharp blow on the raised handle of the slate ripper with a ball-peen hammer *(right)*.

◆ After cutting the nails, slide out the broken piece without disturbing adjacent slates or tiles.

If you do not have a slate ripper, wrap one end of a long hacksaw blade with thick tape. Wearing work gloves, cut the nails with the other end.

INSTALLING REPLACEMENTS

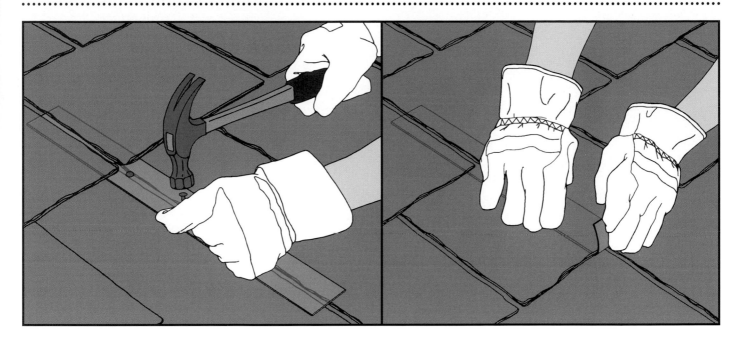

Securing a replacement slate.

◆ Cut a 2-inch-wide strip of metal flashing long enough to extend several inches under the course above the replacement slate and about an inch below it.
◆ Nail the strip to the roof through the joint in the course that underlies the replacement *(above, left)*. If necessary, seat each nail with a punch. Coat the nailheads with roofing cement.
◆ Slide the new slate into position and bend the projecting metal strip up and over the bottom edge of the new slate *(above, right)*. Seal it to the slate with roofing cement so that snow and ice do not dislodge it.

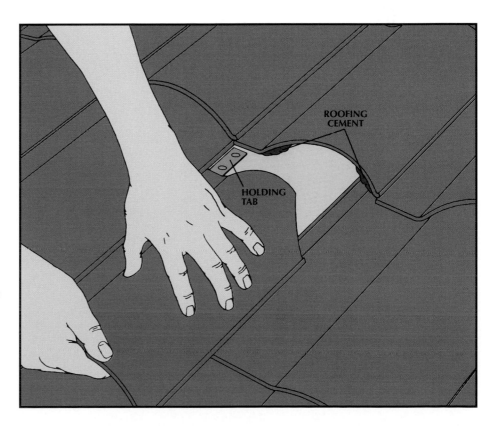

Replacing a tile.

◆ Nail a holding tab like the one used for a slate *(above)* to the roof where the flat part of the new tile will rest.
◆ Put dabs of roofing cement over the nailheads and underneath the tile in the overlying course, where the edges of the new tile will slide.
◆ Slide the new tile into position and bend the holding tab up and around its bottom edge. Seal the exposed tab in position with roofing cement.

Replacing a wood shingle.

◆ Finish removing all the remnants of the damaged shingle, splitting it with a chisel if necessary.

◆ Cut the replacement shingle $\frac{1}{2}$ inch narrower than the space it will fill, to allow for expansion. If the shingle is too long, trim the excess length from the thin end.

◆ With a hammer and wood block, tap the shingle upward, but stop when the bottom edge is $\frac{1}{4}$ inch below the others in its course.

◆ Toenail two galvanized roofing nails just below the edge of the overlying course, making sure the nailheads are even with the shingle surface—not recessed into it, which can cause splitting. Dab roofing cement on the nailheads.

◆ Tap the shingle into place, so that the nailheads lie just under the edge of the overlapping shingles.

DRIP EDGES AND GUTTERS

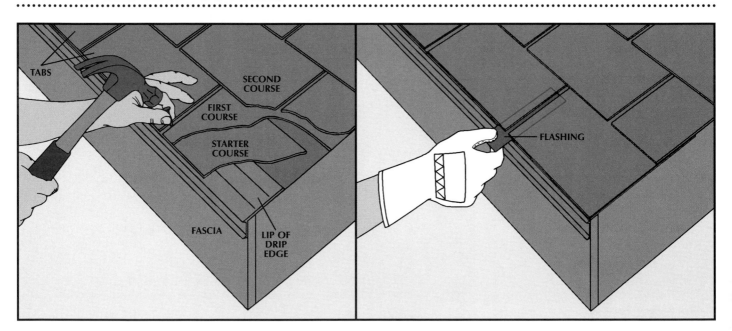

Adding a drip edge.

The fascia, a board running across the rafter ends at the eave, can rot if water soaks it. You can retrofit a metal drip edge to an asphalt-shingle roof by following these steps:

◆ Working on a warm day, when shingles are most pliable, slide the lip of a preformed metal drip edge under the shingles at the eave. The front panel of the drip edge should be about $\frac{1}{4}$ inch in front of the fascia board.

◆ Drive roofing nails between the tabs of the first course of shingles, through the underlying starter course and the drip edge, and into the sheathing (above, left).

◆ Cover the nailheads with roofing ce-

ment. Slide a 2-inch-wide strip of flashing over them, under the first course of shingles and slightly under the second (above, right).

If you then install a gutter as well, slide the upper part of the gutter's back edge behind the drip edge before securing the gutter in place.

94

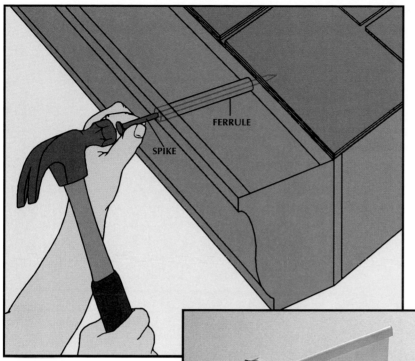

Taking the sag out of a gutter.

When pooling water indicates that a gutter has sagged out of alignment, adjust the gutter slope.

◆ Remove the hardware that supports the sagging portion.

◆ Reposition the gutter so it will drain; one rule of thumb is $\frac{1}{4}$ inch of incline for each 4 feet of run.

◆ Reattach the gutter. Secure metal gutters with spikes and ferrules (tubelike spacers) at the rafter ends, which are indicated by vertical lines of nailheads in the fascia; drive the spike through the gutter, then through the ferrule and into the rafter end *(left)*.

Vinyl gutters require mounting brackets *(photograph)*. Mark the new position, take down the gutter, install the brackets, and put the gutter in place.

Replacing a rusted section.

◆ Use a hacksaw to cut away a steel gutter section that has rusted through.

◆ Spread roofing cement inside the cut ends on each side of the opening.

◆ Slip in a new piece of gutter long enough to rest on the cut ends.

◆ Drill at least four holes through the overlapping ends of the old and new gutter sections *(right)*.

◆ Drive sheet-metal screws into the holes to secure the sections.

◆ If the crimped front edges of the old and new sections do not fit tightly, use tin snips to cut the crimp off the ends of the new section.

◆ Before painting the new section, etch the surface with a half-vinegar, half-water solution.

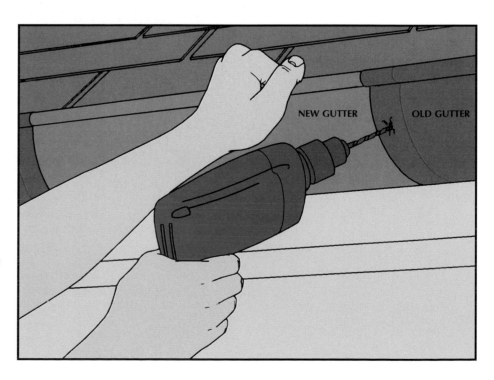

REINFORCING THE ROOF FRAME

Supporting sagging rafters.

One way to prevent a roof sag from worsening is to brace all of the rafters in the sagging area—plus an additional rafter to each side—against the joists below.

◆ Midway between the ridge and eave, nail a 2-by-6 brace at a right angle to each rafter *(right)*.

◆ Nail the other end to the side of the corresponding joist.

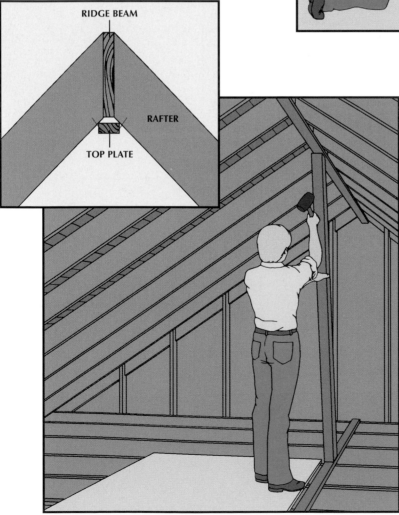

Strengthening the ridge beam.

You can brace a sagging ridge beam where there is a bearing wall under it on the floor below as follows:

◆ First, check that the wall is directly below the ridge beam by hanging a plumb bob from the beam to the attic floor; make sure the wall top plate is centered at the point indicated by the plumb bob. Also check that the wall runs the length of the ridge beam.

◆ Nail a 2-by-4 top plate to the underside of the ridge beam or, if necessary, to the undersides of the rafters *(inset)*. Directly below it, nail a 2-by-4 bottom plate across the joists.

◆ Measure the distance between the two plates and cut a 4-by-4 post that will fit tightly.

◆ Rest one end of the post on the bottom plate directly over a joist, angle the top end against the top plate, and tap the post into a vertical position with a heavy mallet *(left)*.

◆ Plumb the post with a carpenter's level, then toenail the post to the top and bottom plates.

◆ Install the remaining posts in the same way, spacing them every 8 to 10 feet along the length of the ridge.

Traditionally, damage to walls and other surfaces is repaired by filling or coating them with a like material. But many homeowners prefer a fiberglass patch for some of these repairs. Instead of filling cracks, it bridges them, and because it remains somewhat pliable, it keeps the damage from recurring.

Superior Versatility: These patching materials, which can be used almost anywhere except floors and other walkways, are suitable for both indoor and outdoor repairs. They come in a convenient kit that includes fiberglass tape, an acrylic compound to hold it in place, and a plastic applicator. For patching inside corners, you'll need to add a flexible, triangular implement called a cornering tool *(page 99)*.

Acrylic compound can't be sanded, however, so these materials are most appropriate in places where a rough finish is acceptable. In the living spaces of a house, you can make a less obvious patch with self-adhesive fiberglass tape and conventional joint compound *(overleaf)*.

Surface Preparation: Before a fiberglass patch is applied, any deep holes must be filled. Use the acrylic compound or another filler, such as spackling, that is appropriate for the material being patched. Make sure the surface is clean and dry. Scrape away any loose paint or, in the case of metal, remove rust or corrosion with a wire brush. Powdery surfaces, such as concrete or plaster, should be wiped with a damp rag. If they still feel dusty when dry, it is necessary to varnish them.

The Final Coat: Apply the last coat of compound as smoothly as possible unless you are patching concrete or stucco. In that case, stipple the compound with a brush or textured roller to match the surrounding surface. The fiberglass patch can be painted after drying for 24 hours.

⚠️ **CAUTION** *Turn off nearby pilot flames or gas burners before opening the acrylic compound, and open windows if working indoors.*

TOOLS

Paint scraper	Cornering tool
Wire brush	Paintbrush ($2\frac{1}{2}$" or
Scissors	smaller)

PATCHING A FLAT SURFACE

1. Applying the compound.
◆ With the plastic applicator that comes with the fiberglass patching kit, spread the acrylic compound evenly over the crack *(right)*. Cover the crack and the wall around it to a width 2 inches greater than that of the fiberglass tape and at least 1 inch beyond each end of the crack.
◆ Cut the fabric with scissors to the length of the crack plus 2 inches.
◆ With your fingers, press the fabric lightly onto the compound. When a crack is too wide for one piece of fabric, apply additional compound to the edge of the first piece and overlap it at least $1\frac{1}{2}$ inches with the second piece.

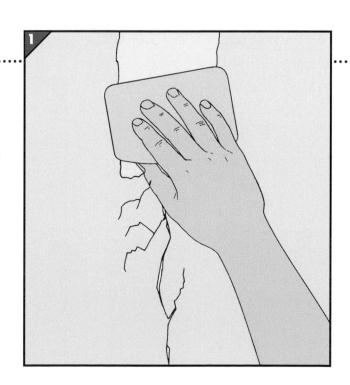

CAMOUFLAGING A REPAIR

Self-adhesive fiberglass tape is ideal for mending a crack where the fix must be unnoticeable. This material is covered with ordinary wallboard joint compound. Unlike the acrylic material used with nonadhesive fiberglass tape, joint compound can be sanded to a smooth finish.

Begin a repair by pressing the tape directly over the crack. If you need more than one width of tape to cover a wide crack, overlap the pieces about $\frac{1}{2}$ inch. Apply two coats of joint compound with a dry-wall knife, then sand the patch to feather the edges.

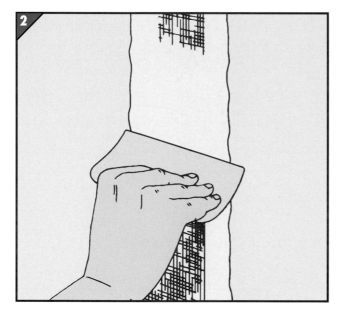

2. Embedding the fabric.
◆ Hold the applicator almost at a right angle to the wall, across the center of the tape.
◆ Working from the center toward the ends, scrape the applicator over the tape to push it well into the compound *(left)*.
◆ After embedding the cloth, let the compound dry.

3. Smoothing the final coat.
◆ Apply a second coat of compound, then sweep the applicator lightly from the center of the patch to its sides *(right)*.
◆ Go over the patch two or three times to smooth it and feather the edges of the compound.

On textured surfaces, stipple the final coat with a brush or paint roller.

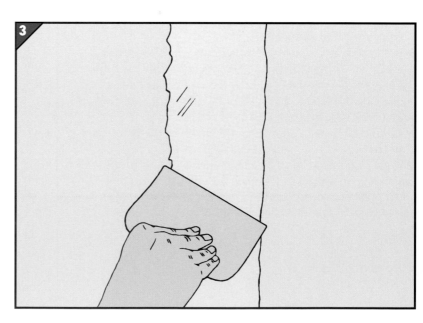

SPECIAL TECHNIQUES FOR CORNERS AND CURVES

Patching an inside corner.
◆ After applying the first coat of compound, fold the tape in half lengthwise and press it into the corner.
◆ Embed the fabric with the point of a cornering tool *(right)*. First work up and down the corner, then smooth the fabric toward the edges on each side.

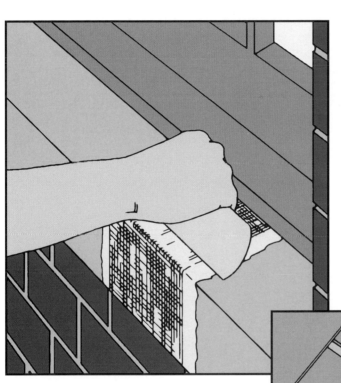

Patching an outside corner.
◆ After spreading the compound, stretch the fabric smoothly around the corner from one surface to the next.
◆ Embed the fabric by working from the corner to the edges on both sides *(above)*.
◆ Once the compound is dry, apply a second coat. Smooth the patch with light strokes and feather the compound's edges.

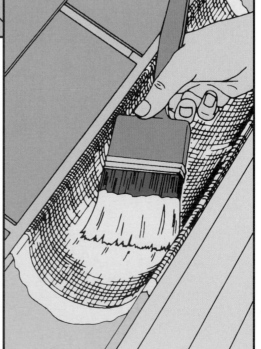

Patching a curved surface.
For contours where the applicator cannot reach—the inside of a rusted gutter, for example—you can apply the compound and embed the fabric with a paintbrush *(left)*. The patch will not be as smooth as one applied to a flat surface, but it will seal tightly and form a weatherproof skin.

The exterior walls of a house, no less than the roof, must be kept in good condition to protect against the elements. Masonry walls—brick or stone—provide good weather protection but benefit from application of a waterproofing sealer *(page 103)*. Wood sidings require more attention: Except for such naturally rot-resistant woods as cedar and redwood, they must be periodically repainted to repel water effectively.

Protecting Wood Exteriors: Before repainting a wood house, wash it with a garden hose, a mild detergent, and a scrub brush where needed. Scrape off loose or peeling paint, then examine the entire surface. Dark stains, blistering, cracking, and rust streaks around nailheads all indicate that moisture is getting into the wood. Unless the source is found and fixed, the new paint will not last.

Cracks and splits can be filled with caulk; large breaks may need to be packed with foam backer rods first *(opposite, top)*. A board with a slight degree of rot can be saved if you scrape it bare, let it dry for several days, and apply wood preservative. Any board with significant rot must be replaced *(page 109)*.

Dealing with Brick: Brick is a low-maintenance material. Unless brick walls have deteriorated badly, repointing is the only repair that they are likely to need *(page 123)*. Even cleaning is optional. Masons once believed that dirt and other pollutants gradually ate into the surface, but research suggests that in some cases grime can actually form a protective shell.

To clean fragile, old brick, try flushing it with a garden hose. Otherwise rent a pressure washer, which blasts off dirt with a high-velocity jet of water. A unit that generates a pressure of less than 1,500 pounds per square inch is preferable. If you can get only a higher-pressure machine, use the widest nozzle orifice that will work.

Brick walls that have been painted should be repainted—never sandblasted. Sandblasting would seriously damage the surface of the brick.

⚠️ **CAUTION** *Consult page 10 for advice on testing for and working with lead paint.*

⚠️ **CAUTION** *Work carefully from a well-secured ladder. Place materials in a bucket, hung from a rung of an extension ladder with a hook.*

⚠️ **CAUTION** *Cover any nearby shrubbery and windows whenever spraying chemicals.*

TOOLS

WOOD	MASONRY
Replaceable-blade paint scraper	Garden hose
Heat gun	Pressure washer (gas-powered)
Wood chisel	Stiff-fiber brush
Caulking gun	Paintbrush
Paintbrush	Wire brush with scraper attachment
Stiff-bristled, nonmetallic brush	Tank-type deck sprayer

MATERIALS

WOOD	
Backer rod	Medium-grade sandpaper or steel wool
Acrylic latex caulk (exterior-use)	
Stain killer (exterior-use, oil- or alcohol-based)	**MASONRY** Detergent Paint remover Waterproofing sealer
Oxalic acid	Turpentine

SAFETY TIPS

Protect your eyes with goggles when chipping old caulk. Wear goggles, a cap, and long sleeves when applying paint remover or spraying chemicals.

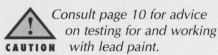

PREPARING WOOD SIDING FOR PAINT

Removing old paint.
Using a replaceable-blade paint scraper and applying pressure on the blade with the heel of one hand as you work, scrape in the direction of the wood's grain to remove loose or peeling paint. If the paint is resistant, you can speed the job with a heat gun *(page 43)*.

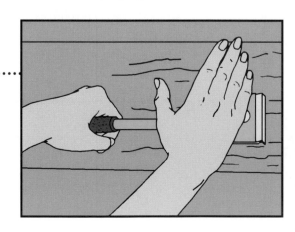

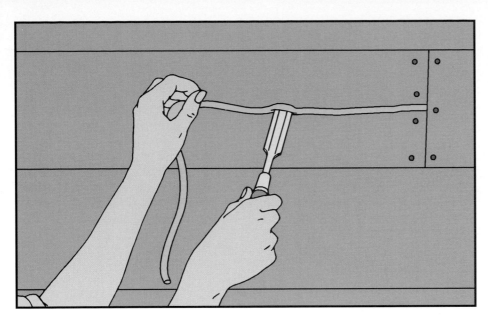

Filling cracks with backer rod.

◆ Insert one end of a strip of backer rod into the widest part of the crack. (Use additional rods as needed.)

◆ Working along the length of the crack, jam the backer rod tightly into the opening with a wood chisel *(left)*. Pack the crack to within $\frac{1}{2}$ inch of the surface.

◆ Cover the backer rod with acrylic latex caulk to create a smooth painting surface.

Caulking the joints.

◆ Put a tube of caulk into a caulking gun and slice off the tip of the tube to make an opening about $\frac{1}{4}$ inch in diameter.

◆ Starting in an unobtrusive spot (under a window sill or above a door), pull the trigger of the gun to about a 45-degree angle and drag the tip of the gun slowly along the joint so that the bead of caulk fills but does not overflow the joint. If the caulk does not flow smoothly, warm the tube slightly over a heat source.

◆ Release the trigger just before reaching the end of the seam.

◆ With a wet finger or a damp cloth, bed the caulking compound into the joint and give a slightly concave shape to its surface.

◆ Wipe off any excess caulking material with a wet cloth.

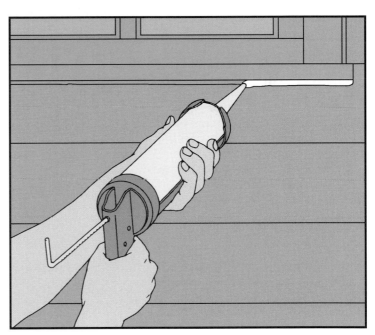

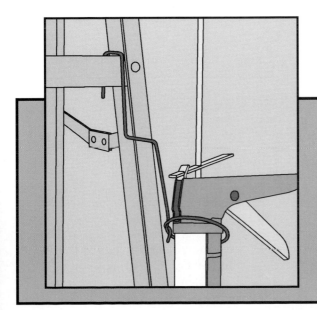

A Wire Holster for a Caulking Gun

To keep a caulking gun close at hand when working on a ladder, create a holsterlike hook like the one at left. Wrap one end of about 22 inches of coat-hanger wire in a half-knot around the neck of the gun, just underneath the base of the trigger. Extend the rest of the wire straight up, then inward the width of a side rail, then up and around to form a hook that will go over a ladder rung.

TRICKS OF THE TRADE

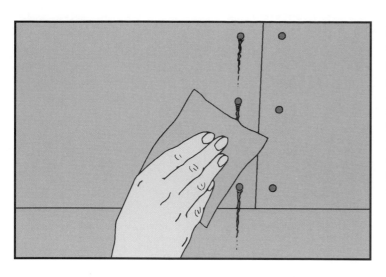

Removing nail rust.

◆ With medium-grade sandpaper, sand a rust-stained area by hand until all of the rust is removed.
◆ Repeat the process on the nailheads themselves to remove any built-up rust.
◆ Coat the nailheads and the area around them with an oil- or alcohol-based stain killer, suitable for exterior use.

If rust has penetrated so deeply that sanding would remove too much wood, try bleaching the stain with oxalic acid, which is available at paint stores. Apply it with a stiff-bristled, non-metallic brush.

SURFACE CLEANING FOR MASONRY

Operating a pressure washer.

◆ With a garden hose, connect the unit to your house cold-water supply.
◆ Determine the greatest distance from which dirt and pollutants can be removed: With brick that seems sturdy, begin by holding a 25-degree nozzle orifice attachment 3 feet away from the surface; if the masonry is fragile, start farther back, or use a wider nozzle at an indirect angle.
◆ For reaching under eaves, extension rods such as the one shown at right are available with some units.

 CAUTION *Do not operate a pressure washer from a ladder.*

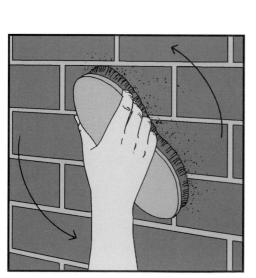

Scrubbing brick.

Walls that are badly soiled with soot or other pollutants may need to be scrubbed. As a cleaning solution, use a handful of detergent in a bucket of cold water. With a stiff-fiber brush, scrub in a circular motion to avoid washing old, fragile mortar out of the joints between bricks; do not scrub back and forth along a mortar line. After the scrubbing, rinse the wall well with clean water.

Applying paint remover.
◆ After wetting the wall, brush on paint remover in one direction *(left)*.
◆ Let the stripper work for 15 to 30 minutes.
◆ Rinse the stripper thoroughly with a garden hose—or, if necessary, a pressure washer.

Scraping and brushing.
To remove spots of paint that dripped onto brick when wood trim above was painted, use a tool with a wire brush on one end and a scraper on the other. Flip the tool every few strokes, first brushing and then scraping; avoid the mortar joints *(right)*. Even when used with care, the brush may leave the mortar joints with depressions that will need filling.

Sealing damaged brick.
Apply sealer when the air and surface temperature are 50°F or higher and the walls have been dry for 3 full days. If the sealer is put on damp walls, salt deposits will be trapped behind the brick, eventually causing it to crumble.
◆ Fill a tank-type deck sprayer with a waterproofing solution, available at most paint and hardware stores. Select the lowest possible pressure, with the nozzle set for a coarse spray.
◆ Beginning under the eaves, flood the surface evenly *(left)*. Hold the nozzle close to the wall for maximum control. As you spray, let the sealer run down 5 to 12 inches. Dab off any buildup with a brush. Cover every square inch of the surface, including all joints; otherwise, water may enter the wall and become trapped by the silicone.
◆ Clean the deck sprayer by running turpentine through it; flush the turpentine out with water.

Patching Holes in Stucco

Properly applied and cured, stucco is a nearly indestructible wall covering. It dries concrete hard and has no seams or joints to admit water. Over the years, however, stucco can develop small cracks or holes. Water entering through the damaged areas can then rot the supporting wood structure within. Patching such flaws in the stucco is straightforward, but it takes several days because of the required drying intervals.

For this type of small repair, buy stucco in ready-mixed dry form. Add just enough water to give it a uniform, plastic texture that leaves a fairly heavy residue on your glove but still holds together when it is picked up and squeezed. If the stucco mix begins to dry out as you work, chop it and mix it with a trowel to restore its proper consistency. Do not add more water; that would weaken the mixture.

It is best to patch a stucco wall on a humid, overcast day, moderate in temperature. In any case, the night before you apply the stucco, wet down the area to be patched, and spray it again just before you begin.

 TOOLS

Trowel
Old scrub brush
Putty knife
Garden hose

 SAFETY TIPS

Wear goggles when you pour out the dry mix, which contains lime. Protect your hands with gloves as you work with wet stucco.

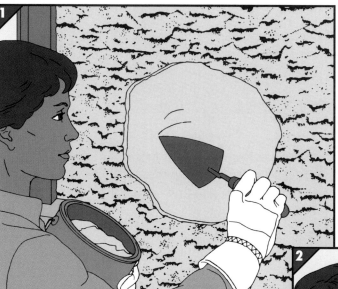

1. Filling a hole or crack.
◆ Clean away any loose debris with an old scrub brush. Widen narrow cracks to about an inch with a putty knife, taking care not to deepen the crack.
◆ Apply stucco with a trowel to within $\frac{1}{4}$ inch of the surface of the wall *(left)*. Tamp the stucco in firmly as you work.

If the wall has been exposed down to the lath, apply this level of the stucco in two layers, letting the first set overnight.

2. Smoothing the patch.
◆ An hour after completing the underlying stucco, smooth the surface with a small block of wood, using a circular motion *(right)*.
◆ Dampen the patch with light spray from a garden hose every 12 hours for the next 48 hours.
◆ Let the stucco dry completely before adding the finish coat; depending on the climate and the thickness of the patch, drying may take 2 to 5 days.

3. Applying the final coat.

◆ Dampen the wall.

◆ Trowel on a finish coat of stucco $\frac{1}{8}$ to $\frac{3}{4}$ inch thick, depending on the texture you must match.

◆ Let the stucco set until it just yields to finger pressure, then add the design. You can produce the basic English-cottage texture at left by applying thick blobs of stucco over a thin base, then using a twisting motion with a triangular trowel. For other styles, see the box below.

MATCHING THE STUCCO PATTERN

Three common alternatives to the stucco design shown above can also be produced with a minimum of equipment. To create the modern-American pattern *(below, left)*, scrape a block of wood downward over the damp surface of a thin coat of stucco. For a spattered effect *(below, center)*, fill a short broom or brush with stucco and hit it against a stick so that it sprays the stucco onto the wall. To make the travertine pattern, first jab a whisk broom repeatedly into a thick coat of stucco *(right, top)*, then smooth out the high points with a wood block or finishing trowel *(right, bottom)*.

MODERN-AMERICAN

SPATTERED

TRAVERTINE

Restoring Outside Walls

Although bared to the elements, exterior walls are the least trouble-prone structural part of a house and can usually be kept sound with preventive maintenance *(pages 100-103)*. When water damage occurs, it is often caused by a roof or gutter leak that has allowed moisture to accumulate on the undersides of exterior boards. In such a case, find and patch the leak *(pages 90-95)* before you make wall repairs. Also check window sills: Water collecting on their horizontal surfaces can lead to rot.

Fixing a Damaged Sill: Correct minor defects in a window sill by scraping away damaged wood, soaking the boards with a wood preservative, and applying a fiberglass patch *(pages 97-99)*. For damage that is more extensive, cover the sill with aluminum sheathing as shown on pages 107 to 108, and then paint it to match the house. You may need to restore the original shape of the sill with wood putty before installing either type of patch.

Rotted Exterior Boards: Check for rot or other damage to wood siding as described on page 100. It is easy enough to replace a few small rotted sections of siding *(page 109)*. Overhang repairs are also straightforward *(pages 108-109)*, although you may need scaffolding to stand on if the overhangs are wide. Patch any holes in the fascia—the board that covers rafter ends—and in the soffit, the board on the underside of the overhang, if only to keep out birds and squirrels. Paint the backs of replacement boards to prevent future rot.

Repairs to Brick Walls: In a masonry wall, the most common failure is the deterioration of mortar. Chip decaying mortar out of the joints and refill them with new mortar *(page 123)*.

Crumbling mortar joints over a door or window opening can cause bricks to sag or even fall out of the wall. As shown on pages 110 to 111, you can reinstall the bricks and strengthen the opening with a pair of L-shaped steel lintels. You may have to remove trim molding and knock out some plaster on the interior wall before you can replace interior courses of bricks. If you must use new bricks to replace broken or missing ones, try to match the old in size and color. When you finish the repair, scrub mortar stains from the bricks with muriatic acid.

 TOOLS

SILL REPAIRS
Scissors
Tin snips
Caulking gun
Hammer
Rubber mallet
Paintbrush

OVERHANG AND SIDING REPAIRS
Electric drill with $\frac{1}{2}$" bit
Saber saw
Keyhole saw
Wood chisel
Backsaw
Hacksaw blade

MASONRY REPAIRS
Cold chisel or brick set
Maul (4-lb.)
Stiff wire brush
Trowel
Jointer
Bricklayer's hammer

 MATERIALS

SILL REPAIRS
Heavy paper
Aluminum sheathing (0.019")
Butyl caulk
Roofing nails (1$\frac{1}{2}$")
Metal preparative
Paint

OVERHANG AND SIDING REPAIRS
Pressure-treated lumber
Galvanized screws
Wood strips (1 x 4)
Wood putty (exterior-grade)
Wedges
Wood blocks
Common nails
Wood siding

MASONRY REPAIRS
Steel lintels
Metal primer
Bricks
Mortar mix
Muriatic acid

SAFETY TIPS

Protect your eyes with goggles when you hammer nails, saw into old wood, or cut a brick. When cutting pressure-treated lumber, wear a dust mask, and wash your hands thoroughly afterward. Don a hard hat if you are removing or installing bricks overhead. Always wear gloves and a long-sleeved shirt to protect your skin when working with mortar or any lime, and put on rubber gloves and goggles when you work with muriatic acid.

SHEATHING FOR A WOOD SILL

WINDOW STOOL

WINDOW JAMB

EAR

PAPER TEMPLATE

FOLD

FOLD

CUT

1. Making templates.
◆ With scissors and heavy paper, make a template to cover each end of a damaged window sill *(left),* fitting the paper against the jamb and around that ear of the sill and reaching from the window stool to the underside of the sill.
◆ Unfold each template *(inset).* Tape a rectangular piece between the two that establishes the correct distance between the jambs.
◆ Transfer the pattern of the assembled paper templates—including the interior cut made at each end—onto 0.019-inch aluminum sheathing *(page 50).* Cut the aluminum with tin snips and check the fit against the window.

2. Caulking the edges.
With a caulking gun, lay a bead of butyl caulk on and around the sill wherever the edges of the metal sheathing will lie—along the window stool, the jambs, the siding, and the underside of the sill.

3. Securing the sheathing.
◆ Position the metal sheathing on the sill and press it into the bead of caulk along the stool, the jambs, and the siding.
◆ Secure the sheathing with $1\frac{1}{2}$-inch roofing nails at 4-inch intervals along the joint of the window sill and stool *(left).*
◆ Nail the metal in place along the jamb edges and the top of each ear.

4. Fitting the sheathing.

◆ Using a rubber mallet, bend the sheathing flaps down over the ears, with the tabs at the ends folded under the ears. Bend the sections produced by the interior cuts around the sill face and secure them with nails.

◆ Bend the long part of the sheathing over the face of the sill *(left),* then up under the bottom.

◆ Nail the folded-under edges to the bottom of the sill.

◆ Seal small gaps with caulk.

◆ Clean the aluminum with metal preparative (available in paint stores) and paint the sheathing with a paint recommended for use on aluminum.

REPAIRING ROTTED CORNICES

FASCIA

1. Cutting away damaged wood.

Replace a rotted section of a fascia or soffit as follows:

◆ Locate nearby rafter ends and lookouts *(below)* by the position of nailheads in the fascia and soffit. (Lookouts are not always present.)

◆ Avoiding rafters and lookouts, drill a $\frac{1}{2}$-inch pilot hole just beyond the area of damaged wood.

◆ Insert the blade of a saber saw or keyhole saw in the hole and cut through the board *(left).*

◆ Make a second saw cut on the other side of the damaged area.

◆ Use a chisel as necessary to complete the two cuts, then pry out the damaged section of board.

2. Doubling damaged rafter ends.

◆ Where a rafter end has rotted, cut a piece of pressure-treated lumber to match the shape of the end of the rafter, long enough to reach back to sound wood.

◆ Nail the new piece alongside the rotted end *(right).*

If a horizontal lookout board is in the way, remove it in order to nail on the new rafter end. Replace rotted lookouts with new lumber cut to the same dimensions.

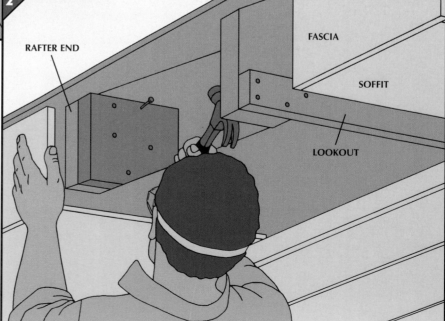

RAFTER END

FASCIA

SOFFIT

LOOKOUT

3. Attaching new boards.

◆ Using galvanized screws, attach a 1-by-4 wood strip that will overlap the back of the new joint at each edge of the sound part of the fascia or soffit *(left)*.

◆ Screw a replacement section to the strips and nail it to any rafter ends or lookouts that it crosses.

◆ Seal the joint at each end with exterior-grade wood putty before you paint.

REPLACING DAMAGED SECTIONS OF SIDING

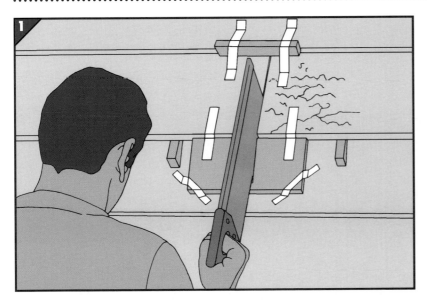

1. Cutting out damaged clapboards.

◆ Tap wedges under a damaged section of clapboard siding to separate it from the piece below.

◆ Tape wood blocks to the boards located above and below the damaged area to protect them as you saw.

◆ Cut through the damaged section with a backsaw *(left)*.

If the siding is made of flush boards, cut out damaged wood with a hammer and chisel and replace it with new wood, using the techniques explained on pages 55 to 56 for repairing floorboards.

2. Finishing the cut.

◆ Move the wedges to the top of the damaged piece to raise the clapboard above.

◆ Finish the cuts, using a keyhole saw with the blade reversed *(right)*.

◆ Wrap one end of a hacksaw blade with tape and use the other end to cut through any nails under the damaged piece.

◆ Remove the piece.

◆ Replace it with a new clapboard, driving nails through the lower part just above the top of the clapboard below.

If there is no sheathing beneath the siding, fasten new siding to old with the technique shown above for attaching a new fascia or soffit board.

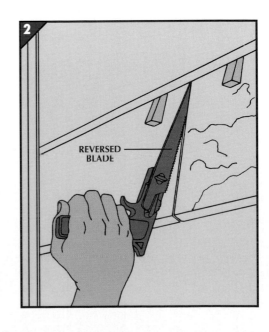

REVERSED BLADE

SUPPORTS FOR A MASONRY OPENING

1. Making the shoulders.

◆ Paint two lintels with metal primer.
◆ With a cold chisel or brick set and a maul, remove two courses of brick above the door or window opening as well as isolated cracked bricks in the course above. (If the damage is extensive, consult a bricklayer.) Also remove enough brick and mortar in these courses on either side to make a ledge, called a shoulder, that is at least half a brick long on each side.
◆ Clean mortar dust from the shoulder bricks with a stiff wire brush.
◆ Dampen the shoulder bricks with water and cover them with a bed of mortar about $\frac{1}{8}$ inch thick.

2. Setting the lintel.

In the case of a wall that has a cavity between the face course and the backing course of bricks, position the lintels on the shoulders so that each vertical leg is slightly to the cavity side of the course of bricks below it. Press the lintels into the mortar so that the surface of each horizontal leg is flush with the top of the mortar joint beside it.

If there is no cavity, hold the lintels back to back as you press them into the mortar *(right)*. Align the joint between the vertical legs of the lintels with the mortar joint between the face and backing courses.

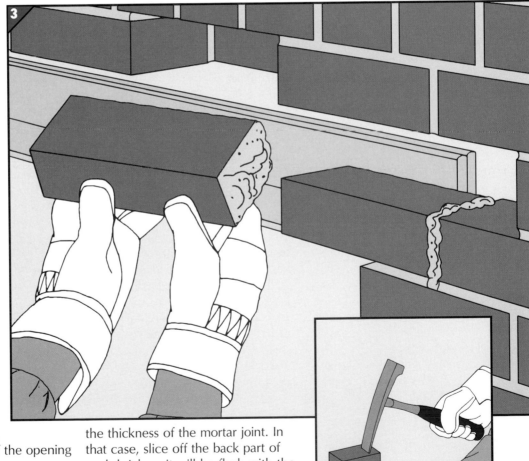

3. Replacing the bricks.

When there is a cavity between the two wall courses, proceed as follows:

◆ Increase the thickness of the mortar at each side of the lintel to $\frac{3}{8}$ inch.

◆ Apply mortar to the end of a brick; lay the brick so that it is partly on the lintel and partly on the mortared lower brick and tamp it into place.

◆ Lay the rest of the course; slide in mortared bricks for the course above.

◆ Repeat from the inside of the opening on top of the other lintel.

◆ Pack more mortar into the joints with the edge of a trowel, adding a thin joint in front of the lintel above each shoulder. Finish the joints *(page 123)*.

If there is no wall cavity, the thickness of the vertical lintel legs may exceed the thickness of the mortar joint. In that case, slice off the back part of each brick so it will be flush with the surrounding bricks, striking the brick at one end and then the other with the blade of a bricklayer's hammer *(inset)*. Use the blade to clean off rough spots on the cut edges. Practice this technique on broken bricks before cutting new ones.

Correcting Floor Sags

Some structural faults in a floor are obvious; others show up only after a heavy object has burdened the floor for a few weeks. Sags in the middle of a floor are typically caused by inadequate support from joists and girders. Sags near an exterior wall, however, indicate damage to major structural parts of the house and require more extensive remedies.

Stabilizing the Floor: You can temporarily firm up small sags and bouncy floors near the middle of a house with beams and posts *(opposite, top)*. To eliminate such sags permanently, jack the floor back to level. Use a screw-type jack, since hydraulic jacks can settle over time. A telescoping house jack works well under floor joists more than 22 inches above the ground, and a bell jack *(page 116)* can serve in a crawlspace that is less than 22 inches high.

If you plan to leave the jack in place—or to substitute a 4-by-4 post—have a concrete footing poured before beginning work. Alternatively, since posts or jacks obstruct movement in a basement, you may prefer to strengthen the floor after raising it by nailing new boards to one or both sides of weak joists. At stairways, reinforce the joints between joists with extra framing. Beneath tubs and heavy radiators, nail solid blocking *(page 53)*.

When jacking a floor, raise it no more than $\frac{1}{4}$ inch a day, and never lift it more than $\frac{1}{2}$ inch without obtaining professional advice.

Girder Problems: A girder low at one end usually indicates crumbling in a girder pocket—the hole in the foundation wall where the girder rests. You can usually jack up the girder and rebuild the pocket with mortar. A sag over a post signals rot or an inadequate footing; have the post replaced with a steel column on a new footing. If the girder dips between posts, you can support it with a permanent jack.

Repairing the Sill: Perhaps the most vulnerable structural element in a wood-frame house is the sill plate *(page 114)*, often attacked by rot or insects. When a section of the sill deteriorates, the floor sags near the exterior wall. Damage often extends into the ends of the joists; in a balloon-framed house, ends of first-floor studs are also vulnerable. To repair or replace any of these parts, you must raise the house $\frac{1}{4}$ inch off the foundation, one side at a time. You can work from the basement to raise a side of the house that is perpendicular to the floor joists *(pages 114-115)*; if it parallels the joists, another method is required *(pages 115-116)*. From that point on, repair techniques are much the same *(pages 116-121)*.

For the replacement sill, buy pressure-treated lumber that closely matches the thickness of the old sill; you can compensate for boards up to $\frac{1}{2}$ inch thinner with a mortar bed atop the foundation wall. In the case of a very old house, which may have sills as much as 8 inches thick, custom-order wood from a sawmill and have it pressure treated.

Lifting the side of a house inevitably invites minor damage. Pipes and ducts can rupture; disconnect the joints of any drain stack within 2 feet of the area to be raised. Plaster walls sometimes crack or buckle; make repairs as shown on pages 46 to 48.

Rotted Board Ends: When you replace part of a sill, also reinforce or replace any end-damaged joists and studs. The header and band joists, which run along the perimeter of the house, are easy to remove; if one is damaged, it is simpler to replace it than to attempt repairs.

Although a solid-masonry house does not have wood studs in the exterior walls *(page 9)*, its joists are vulnerable to rot and insects. Repair and reinforce rotted joist ends in such a house as shown on pages 119 to 120.

⚠ **CAUTION** *Do not jack the side of a solid-masonry house or one with a masonry veneer—a layer of bricks over wood framing. Cracking of the masonry can result.*

 TOOLS

Hammer
Carpenter's level
Telescoping house jack
Screwdriver
Adjustable wrench
Pry bar
Bell jack

Reciprocating saw
Hacksaw
Saber saw
Cold chisel
Wire brush
Trowel
Maul (4-lb.)
Circular saw
Wood chisel

 MATERIALS

Pressure-treated lumber (4 x 4, 2 x 12, 2 x 8)
Standard lumber (4 x 8, 2 x 6, 2 x 4)
Wood shims
Galvanized common nails ($2\frac{1}{2}$" and $3\frac{1}{2}$")
Lubricating oil

Epoxy glue
Mortar
Anchor-bolt washers
Tie straps (12-gauge steel)
Lag screws ($\frac{1}{2}$" x $3\frac{1}{2}$" and $\frac{1}{2}$" x $4\frac{1}{2}$") and lead shields
Wood preservative

 SAFETY TIPS

Protect your eyes with goggles when hammering nails; supplement these with a dust mask when you operate a power saw or cut away masonry with a chisel. A hard hat is essential whenever you work with unsecured lumber overhead. Work gloves protect your hands when you spread wet mortar.

BRACING A WEAK SPOT

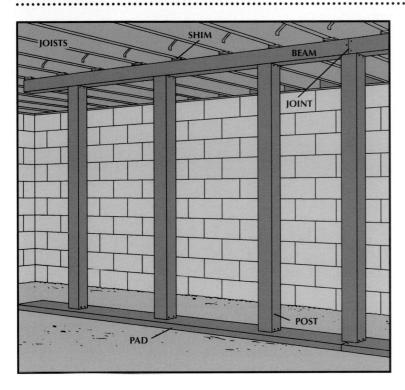

Shoring weak joists.

◆ To brace a sagging floor, make a beam of 10-foot pressure-treated 4-by-4s, laid end to end on the basement floor perpendicular to the joists.

◆ Cut three pressure-treated 4-by-4 posts for each beam section, plus an additional post for each beam joint. Make the posts $5\frac{1}{4}$ inches shorter than the measurement between the floor and the joists at the point of lowest sag.

◆ Toenail three posts to each beam section, one in the center and one 2 feet from each end.

◆ Lay a wood pad for the posts. On a dirt floor, use 10-foot pressure-treated 2-by-12s end to end; on a concrete floor, 12-inch lengths of 2-by-8 will do.

◆ With a helper, set each post-and-beam section on the corresponding pad. Tap pairs of wood shims between the beam and the joists.

◆ Plumb each post with a carpenter's level, then toenail it to the pad.

◆ Drive in the shims.

◆ Insert a post at every beam joint and then toenail the beam sections together.

Jacking a sagging girder.

With a house jack, you can easily straighten a girder that is sagging in the middle.

◆ For a permanent repair, have a concrete footing poured beneath the point of lowest sag.

◆ Set a 3-foot-long 4-by-8 pad on the footing.

◆ Put a telescoping house jack on the pad, extend its upper tube to the girder, and lock the tube with the two steel pins provided. Turn the screw at the bottom until the top of the jack presses snugly against the girder *(right)*.

◆ Plumb the jack with a carpenter's level and nail the flat steel plates at each end to the girder and to the pad.

◆ Jack the girder $\frac{1}{4}$ inch each day—roughly a half-turn of the screw on most

models. If the screw is stiff, oil the threads and slide a pipe over the handle for more leverage. Check the ends of the girder—if they begin to rise, the jack is lifting the entire girder rather than straightening the sag. Stop jacking for a few days and moisten the girder with a garden sprayer to increase its flexibility.

◆ To leave the jack in place, remove the handle; fill the threads with epoxy glue.

If the girder is sagging at a supporting post, set pads on each side of the post and brace the girder with two jacks until you can have the defective post replaced.

LEVELING A FLOOR FROM BELOW

1. Preparing the wall.

If the side of the house is perpendicular to the floor joists, proceed as follows. Otherwise, follow the steps that begin on the next page.

◆ Unscrew nuts and remove washers from any anchor bolts that fasten the sill plate to the foundation; if the sill and joists are connected by metal straps, remove them as well.

◆ Outside the house, use a pry bar to remove a horizontal strip of siding and sheathing wide enough to expose the sill plate, the header joist, and the lower ends of the studs.

If the house has balloon framing *(page 9),* with no header joist and with studs that stand on the sill plate beside the joists, check that the joists and studs are fastened together with at least four $3\frac{1}{2}$-inch nails *(inset);* add extra nails if necessary.

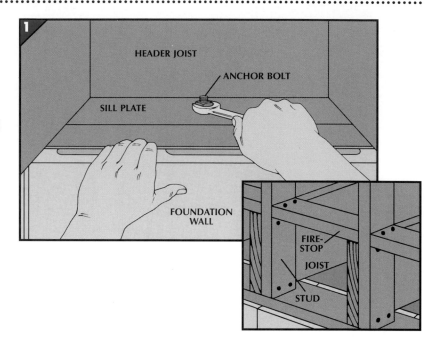

2. Setting up the jack.

◆ At one end of the wall in the basement, toenail a 10-foot 4-by-4 beam to the bottoms of joists. Run the beam parallel with the foundation wall and about 18 inches from it *(left).* As you work, add shims to fill any gaps between joists and beam.

◆ Lay a 10-foot 2-by-12 pad on the floor under the beam.

◆ Plumb a telescoping house jack at the center of the pad and beam, and raise the jack just enough to hold it upright.

3. Jacking the beam.

◆ Raise the jack until the floor above is level, as indicated by a carpenter's level set at a right angle to the wall and directly above the jack *(right).*

◆ When the floor is level, measure the space between the joist bottoms and the top of the foundation wall at points near the jack to gauge the thickness of lumber you need to replace the defective section of sill.

4. Supporting the beam.

◆ Cut a 4-by-4 post to fit between the pad and the beam, alongside the jack.

◆ Plumb the post, tapping it into place with a maul. Shim as needed for a tight fit *(right)*. Remove the jack.

◆ Sight along the beam to determine whether the ends are bowing down from the weight of the house. If so, set up the jack 2 feet from one end of the beam, jack that end level with the center of the beam, and insert another 4-by-4 post there. Jack and support the other end in the same way.

◆ Repeat this procedure the full length of the wall.

◆ Starting at one end of the line of beams, raise the beam another $\frac{1}{4}$ inch at each post and shim the top accordingly.

LIFTING A FLOOR FROM OUTSIDE

STUD

BAND JOIST

SILL PLATE

1. Attaching ledgers.

◆ Prepare the wall for jacking by freeing the anchor bolts, removing any metal straps between the sill and foundation, and taking off some siding and sheathing *(Step 1, opposite page)*.

◆ Check the band joist for rot or other damage.

◆ Working outside the house—and starting at one end of the wall—nail 2-by-6 ledgers, each 10 feet long, to the house. Fasten them to the band joist if it is sound; otherwise nail them to the wall, with the ledger bottoms 3 feet above the sill plate *(left)*.

◆ Add a second layer of ledgers, staggering joints with those in the first layer.

◆ Secure the ledgers with two $\frac{1}{2}$- by $4\frac{1}{2}$-inch lag screws every 16 inches, driving the screws into the band joist or wall studs.

◆ Level the earth near the foundation wall and lay 2-by-12 pads on the ground alongside the foundation. Drive stakes along the outside of the pads to hold them in place.

2. Jacking the ledger wall.

◆ Set a bell jack on the pad, $1\frac{1}{2}$ feet from the end of the wall.

◆ Cut a 4-by-4 to fit between the jack and the bottom of the doubled ledger; have a helper hold the 4-by-4 while you raise the jack. Then jack the ledger up $\frac{1}{4}$ inch.

◆ Cut a 2-by-4 about $\frac{1}{16}$ inch longer than the distance between the ledger and the pad.

◆ Place the top of the 2-by-4 under the ledger so that it touches the wall, and drive the bottom toward the wall with a hammer. The brace should lean toward the wall at an angle of 5 to 10 degrees (inset).

◆ Remove the bell jack.

◆ Jack and support the doubled ledger in the same fashion every 3 to 4 feet.

◆ Raise the entire wall no more than $\frac{1}{4}$ inch at a time until the floor inside is level (page 114, Step 3), then raise it another $\frac{1}{4}$ inch. Each time, work down the wall with the jack, raising the ledger beside each brace and tapping wood shims under the brace.

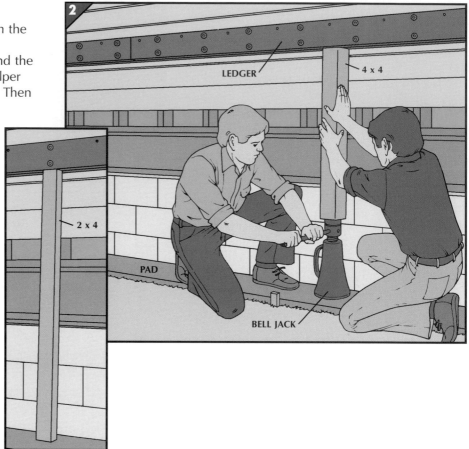

REPLACING PART OF A SILL PLATE

1. Cutting out the damaged section.

◆ With a pry bar, lever the rotted piece of sill slightly away from the header or band joist above it.

◆ Sever the nails that fasten the sill to the header or band joist and to the floor joists. To do so, cut horizontally along the top of the sill with a rented reciprocating saw fitted with a metal-cutting blade (right).

◆ Outside the rotted portion of the sill, cut vertically through the sill midway between two anchor bolts; then make vertical cuts on both sides of each bolt within the rotted section.

◆ Knock out the cut pieces of sill with a hammer.

◆ Inspect the joists that rested on the sill for rot or insect damage. Reinforce or replace any damaged joists (pages 118-119).

If you have a balloon-framed house, proceed similarly. Pry the sill away from the stud bottoms, and in the case of a wall perpendicular to the joists, also pry the sill from the joist ends. Cut the nails fastening the sill to studs and joists; check the stud bottoms and joists for crumbling from rot and insects. Repair damaged stud ends (pages 120-121).

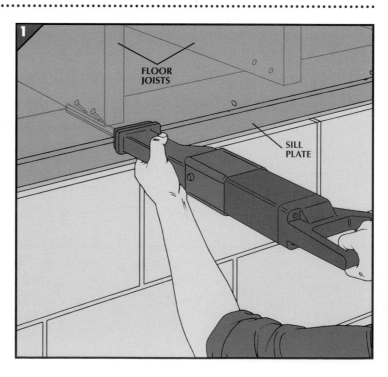

2. Notching the new sill section.

◆ Examine the anchor bolts. Remove any corroded beyond use by cutting halfway through each with a hacksaw or the reciprocating saw, flush with the foundation's top. Then snap the bolt along the cut by hitting the top sideways with a hammer.

◆ Cut a length of sill plate lumber to fill the gap. (When replacing a long section with more than one piece of lumber, cut them so that joints fall midway between anchor bolts.)

◆ Have a helper hold the board on the foundation wall from outside the house while you mark the width of each remaining anchor bolt from inside *(right)*.

◆ At each mark, cut a notch just deep enough for the new sill plate to align with the outer edge of the existing one. Use a saber saw to notch sills up to $1\frac{1}{2}$ inches thick, a reciprocating saw for thicker ones.

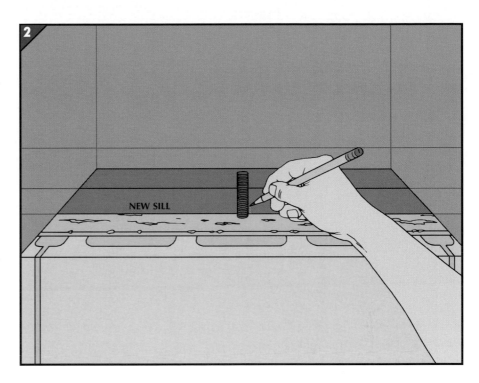

NEW SILL

3. Preparing the foundation.

Skip to the next step if the new sill is as thick as the old one and there is either a sound mortar bed beneath the old sill or no bed at all. Otherwise, proceed as follows:

◆ Chip off all the old mortar with a cold chisel and clean the top of the foundation wall with a wire brush.

◆ Gather spalls—bits of old mortar, brick, or concrete block—to hold the new sill at the correct height and keep it from squeezing the wet mortar out.

◆ Wet the foundation, then spread a new bed of mortar. Every 4 inches, tap a spall into the mortar with the butt of your trowel handle.

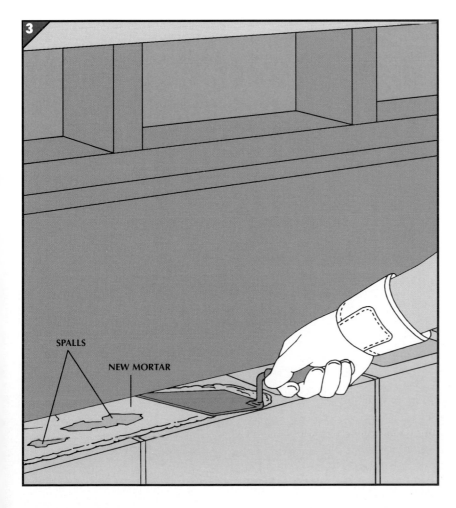

SPALLS

NEW MORTAR

ANCHOR BOLT

TIE STRAP

4. Fastening the new sill.
◆ Slide the new sill section into place around the old anchor bolts *(right)*; if you raised the house with ledgers, slide the lengths of sill behind the braces, then rotate each into place. Where there is new mortar, tap the piece of sill down onto it, matching the angle of the old sill. Let the mortar set for 1 day.

◆ Slide oversized washers over the anchor bolts, then tighten the original nuts securely *(inset, left)*. Squirt some oil on the bolts if the nuts are hard to turn.

◆ Lower the house gradually, $\frac{1}{4}$ inch at a time, by reversing the procedure used to raise it.

◆ Toenail floor joists to the new sill. Do the same for studs in the case of a balloon-framed house.

◆ For every anchor bolt you had to cut off, substitute a twisted 12-gauge steel tie strap *(inset, right)*. If there were no anchor bolts, install a strap at every third joist. Anchor each strap to the foundation with two $\frac{1}{2}$- by $3\frac{1}{2}$-inch lag screws and lead shields. Nail the strap to the joist.

REPAIRS FOR JOISTS IN A FRAME HOUSE

BRIDGING

SPACER

REINFORCING BOARD

DAMAGED JOIST

WOOD BLOCK

Reinforcing a rotted joist.
Before inserting the new sill, repair damaged joist ends as follows:

◆ One side of the joist must be unobstructed; remove any pipes, ducts, or electrical cables that are in the way. Also take out bridging beside the joist; as substitutes, cut 2-by-6 spacers to fit tightly between joists.

◆ Measure the extent of the damage. If it covers more than 2 inches but does not extend past the inner edge of the sill plate, use a supporting board at least one-fourth as long as the joist; longer is better. If the damage reaches beyond the sill but is less than one-tenth the length of the joist, reinforce at least half the length of the joist. More extensive rot requires a reinforcing board the full length of the joist.

◆ Cut a reinforcing board

from lumber the same width as the joist.

◆ Set the new board beside the joist, aligning the ends of both boards and forcing the reinforcement board tightly against the subfloor above it.

◆ Fasten the two together with three or four $3\frac{1}{2}$-inch nails every 16 inches *(left)*.

◆ Knock out the spacers and reinstall the bridging, as well as any ducts, cables, or pipes removed earlier.

A joist corner damaged in an area less than 1 inch high and 2 inches long can be reinforced with a small wood block *(inset)*. After lowering the house onto the new sill plate, chisel away the damaged portion until you reach solid wood. Cut a wood block to fit tightly into the opening and drive it into position, then toenail the block to the joist.

Replacing perimeter joists.

While the house is jacked up, you can replace damaged header and band joists as follows:

◆ In either case, nail 2-by-6 spacers between the floor joists, 5 feet from the foundation, unless there is bracing or bridging near that point.

◆ Working outside, use a reciprocating saw to cut horizontally between the subfloor and the defective header or band joist to free it from the sole plate. Then cut out the rotted section.

◆ When replacing a header joist, knock out the old joist with a 2-by-4 and a maul (right).

◆ Cut a replacement joist to the same dimensions as the rotted section of the old one and fasten it to the end of each floor joist with four $3\frac{1}{2}$-inch nails. For long headers, reinforce any joints that fall between floor joists with a block of joist lumber (inset, top).

To install a new band joist, knock the rotted section free from outside. Slide the new joist into position and support it against the subfloor above, then toenail the joist through the subfloor and into the sole plate. Join segments of a new band joist with a block of joist lumber nailed across the joint (inset, bottom).

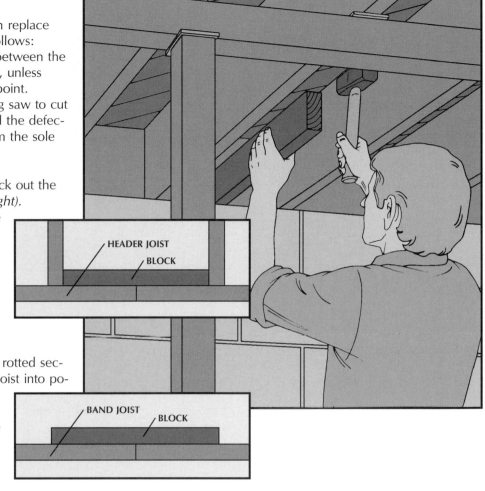

HEADER JOIST
BLOCK

BAND JOIST
BLOCK

REINFORCING JOISTS IN A MASONRY HOUSE

Enlarging a joist pocket.

To accommodate the thickness of a reinforcing board nailed to a joist in a solid-masonry house, jack the joist until it is level (page 114). Then, using a cold chisel and a maul, chip out the masonry on one side of the joist to create a $1\frac{3}{4}$-inch space for the reinforcing board. (Once the board is in place, the extra $\frac{1}{4}$ inch of space can be filled with mortar.)

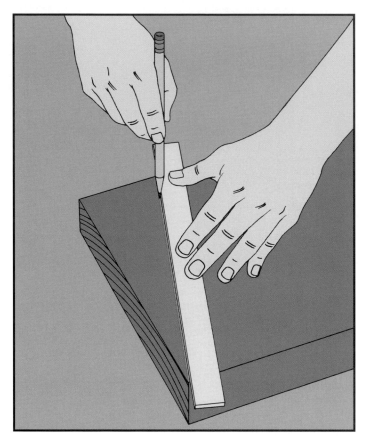

Making a fire cut.

Joists that are set in pockets in a solid-masonry wall have ends that are cut at an angle. In the event of a fire that burns through the center of joists, the angled cuts allow the ends of collapsing joists to fall out of their pockets without catching wall framing at the upper corners, which would pull down the wall.

◆ To cut a reinforcing board for a rotted joist, draw a diagonal line at one end of the board from the lower corner to a point 3 inches in from the upper corner.

◆ Cut the board along this line, then nail it to the old joist as described on page 118.

SPLINTS FOR ROTTED STUDS

1. Cutting off the rotted ends.

After you jack up a balloon-framed house, repair rotted stud ends as follows:

◆ Remove additional siding and sheathing as needed to expose the rotted sections. Knock out the firestops between the studs *(page 114, Step 1, inset)*.

◆ With a reciprocating saw, cut off each stud above the visibly rotted portion, taking care not to cut into joists *(right)*.

◆ Split away the rotted end with a hammer and a wood chisel and drive out protruding nails.

◆ Paint the freshly cut stud end with wood preservative, soaking the wood thoroughly.

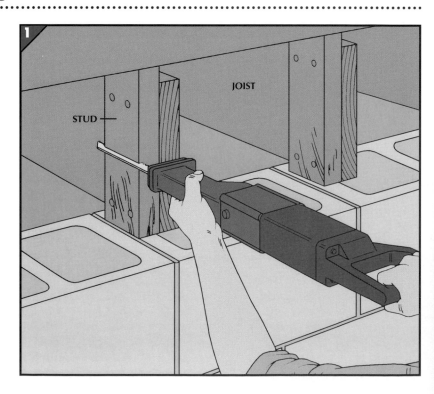

STUD

JOIST

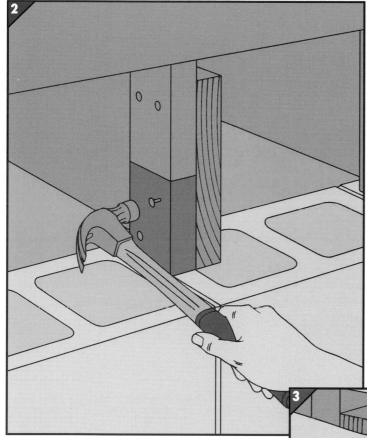

2. Propping up the studs.

◆ For each stud prepared as in Step 1, cut a filler block from lumber trimmed, if necessary, to match the stud dimensions. Make the block tall enough so that its lower end is flush with the bottom of the adjacent joist.

◆ On a side of the house perpendicular to the joists, fasten the blocks to the corresponding joist ends with two $2\frac{1}{2}$-inch nails *(left)*.

If the wall parallels the joists, so that no joist ends are present, reinforce the joints between studs and filler blocks as shown in Step 3, and then nail each filler block to its reinforcing stud.

3. Reinforcing the joint.

◆ Slide a piece of stud stock at least 1 foot long into the wall alongside the stud. A longer board is better if you can maneuver it into position.

◆ Set the lower end of the new board even with the bottom of the filler block, then fasten it to the stud with staggered $3\frac{1}{2}$-inch nails every 6 inches. Attach it to the filler block in the same way.

◆ When all of the rotten stud and joist ends have been repaired, install the new sill plate, and lower the wall as described on page 118.

◆ Toenail the studs and joists to the sill plate and nail new firestops between the studs.

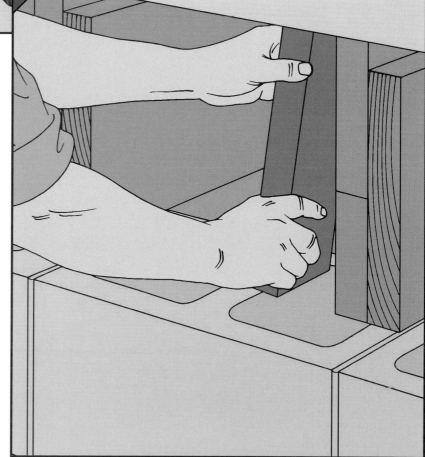

Remedies for Ailing Foundations

Whether built of stone, brick, block, or poured concrete, foundations can develop a multitude of flaws as they age. Small cracks, crumbling mortar, and broken pieces of masonry are structurally harmless. Larger cracks, caused by poor soil drainage or uneven settling of the house *(page 16)*, pose a more serious problem.

Drainage Problems: Before attempting any foundation repairs, check that gutters, downspouts, and grading funnel rainwater away from the house. Correcting poor drainage—whether by repairing existing components or installing a supplemental drain system *(below)*—will help prevent further water damage to a foundation.

Minor Flaws: Dry, stationary cracks can be filled with patching mortar or epoxy. A seeping crack must be patched with hydraulic cement, which hardens even in the presence of water. Use masonry caulk to fill a crack that expands and contracts. If a crack is very large—or reaches the hollow core of a concrete block—pack in expansion-joint material before patching it.

A brick foundation ordinarily has two or three thicknesses, called wythes. When rebuilding a section of the foundation *(page 124)*, you must replace the brick in all of them.

Underpinning Foundations: Buildings may have settled unevenly for a number of reasons; have a structural engineer determine the cause. If the footing is inadequate or absent, you can underpin part or all of the foundation wall *(pages 124-125)*. In a house with a basement, it is usually easiest to work from inside, jackhammering through a concrete floor or digging up a dirt floor. Deal with a crawlspace by hiring a backhoe operator to dig and shore up a trench 4 feet wide all around the house.

 TOOLS

Cold chisel
Maul (4-lb.)
Wire brush
Trowel
Joint filler
Ball-peen hammer
Mason's hawk
Jointer
Tape measure
Shovel

 **MATERIALS**

Mortar mix
Burlap
Polyethylene
 sheeting (6-mil)
2 x 4s
Brick
Steel reinforcing
 bar (No. 4)
Tie wire
Prepackaged
 concrete
1 x 6

 SAFETY TIPS

Shield your eyes with goggles when chiseling or cutting masonry and when working above eye level; protect your hands with gloves when working with caustic mortar and concrete.

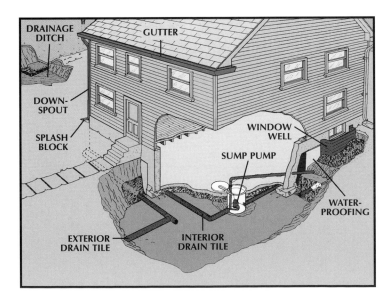

Combating water in the basement.

A system of gutters and downspouts carries water runoff from the roof away from the foundation. Sloped ground adjacent to the foundation also helps. Shored window wells keep water away from basement windows. On a hilly lot, a drainage ditch can divert runoff away from the house.

In some cases, more extensive measures may be required. An exterior drain-tile system installed along the footings prevents water buildup around the foundation, while an interior drain-tile system channels water from under the floor slab to a pit called a sump. A pump there expels the water outdoors. Exterior waterproofing protects against seepage through foundation walls. Consult a professional about the method appropriate for your site.

PATCHING AND POINTING

A dry, stationary crack in concrete.

◆ With a cold chisel and a maul, shape the crack into a groove about $\frac{1}{2}$ inch deep and $\frac{1}{2}$ inch wide. Chisel the sides to make the groove 1 inch wide at the back (inset). Clean the groove with a wire brush.

◆ Spray the groove with water, then use a trowel to fill the crack halfway with patching mortar, mixed according to the manufacturer's instructions. Pack the mortar in tightly with a joint filler.

◆ Wait 1 minute, then fill the groove with mortar.

◆ Smooth the surface of the mortar with the trowel and rub it with a piece of damp burlap to give it a texture matching that of the wall.

◆ Cover the patch with a sheet of plastic propped up by 2-by-4s. Allow the mortar to cure for 3 days, misting it from time to time to keep it damp.

Repointing brick.

◆ Chisel out the old mortar to a depth of 1 inch.

◆ Mix new mortar according to the manufacturer's instructions—or colored to match the old mortar (page 111)—and pile some on a mason's hawk.

◆ Spray the joints with water and press in mortar with a joint filler, holding the hawk just below the joint (right). Scrape off any excess.

◆ When the mortar is firm to the touch, finish the joints to match the rest of the wall by running a jointer or its homemade equivalent along the joints. Use a convex jointer or a teaspoon for a concave shape, a V-jointer or the tip of a trowel for a V-shape, a trowel for flush joints.

◆ Moisten the work occasionally for 3 days while the mortar cures.

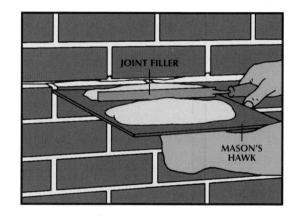

Replacing a broken brick.

◆ Chisel out the brick and mortar (left), taking care not to damage nearby bricks.

◆ Cut 1 inch off the back of a new brick so it will have ample room (page 111).

◆ Moisten the pocket and mortar its back, top, and sides; then mortar the bottom of the pocket to match the thickness of the adjacent joints.

◆ Wet the brick and mortar its back, then place it on a mason's hawk or board and push it into the pocket.

◆ Tap it into position, using the butt of a trowel handle, and press mortar into the joints to fill any gaps.

◆ When the mortar is firm to the touch, finish the joints to match the rest of the wall (above).

To replace a broken concrete block, chisel out the front half of the block, leaving the back half intact, and mortar a solid 4-by-8-by-16 block into the resulting pocket.

Rebuilding part of a foundation.

If the section you plan to replace is more than 2 feet below the floor joists, chisel out the bricks or blocks from an area no more than 3 feet wide, working from top to bottom. The wall will form an arch over the opening to carry the load as you remove the masonry underneath, leaving a zigzag pattern of sound masonry on each side. To remove bricks or blocks less than 2 feet from joists running perpendicular to the wall, support the joist ends with shoring *(page 113, top)* before you remove the masonry.

◆ Chisel out the bricks in the section, one wythe at a time, and clean the exposed surfaces with a wire brush.

◆ Mortar new bricks or blocks in the opening *(page 123)*, adjusting the mortar joints to match the spacing in adjacent masonry.

UNDERPINNING A FOUNDATION WALL

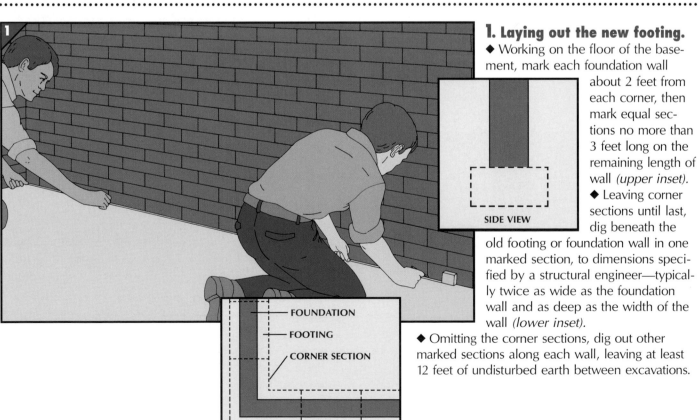

SIDE VIEW

FOUNDATION

FOOTING

CORNER SECTION

TOP VIEW

1. Laying out the new footing.

◆ Working on the floor of the basement, mark each foundation wall about 2 feet from each corner, then mark equal sections no more than 3 feet long on the remaining length of wall *(upper inset)*.

◆ Leaving corner sections until last, dig beneath the old footing or foundation wall in one marked section, to dimensions specified by a structural engineer—typically twice as wide as the foundation wall and as deep as the width of the wall *(lower inset)*.

◆ Omitting the corner sections, dig out other marked sections along each wall, leaving at least 12 feet of undisturbed earth between excavations.

REINFORCING BAR

FOOTING TRENCH

2. Installing reinforcing bars.

◆ Cut six 34-inch-long pieces of No. 4 steel reinforcing bar (rebar) for each excavation.

◆ Drive two pieces about halfway into the dirt at each end of the excavations, placing the bars about 3 inches from the trench bottom and directly below each side of the wall. If necessary, re-move extra dirt on the near side of the excavation to gain access to the far edge of the footing.

◆ Use tie wire to splice the remaining two pieces of rebar lengthwise be-tween protruding pairs of bars in each section.

◆ Dampen the trench section with a hose, then pour in a stiff mixture of concrete, leaving about 2 inches of space between the underside of the old foundation and the top of the new concrete.

◆ Drive a shovel into the concrete re-peatedly to force it under the wall and to eliminate air bubbles.

◆ Cover the concrete with plastic and let it set for a day.

DRY-PACK CONCRETE

POURED CONCRETE

3. Dry-packing the footing.

◆ Make a dry-pack mix-ture of cement, using just enough water for the mix-ture to hold its shape when squeezed.

◆ Trowel the dry-pack into the gap between each footing section and the wall above, then pack it in tightly by driving the end of a 1-by-6 into the gap with a maul.

◆ Add and pack cement until the gaps are completely filled; cover the footing and the dry-pack with plastic sheets and let them cure for 1 week, sprin-kling them with water occasionally.

◆ When the dry-pack has cured for 2 days, repeat Steps 1 and 2 to dig and pour the next set of midwall footing sections, then fill them with concrete as described above.

◆ After you have completed all the midwall sections, dig and fill the corner sections.

◆ If you had to dig through a concrete floor, patch it with new concrete.

INDEX

A

Acrylic compound: for patching, 97

Amperage: evaluating available, 20, 21

Asbestos: handling, 10

Attic, inspecting: 15, 17; and interior inspection, 15; and roof inspection, 17

B

Backer rod: 101

Basement, inspecting: 15-16

Beam: collar, 8; floor support, 113; ridge, 9; sill, 8; summer, 8

Brass: caring for, 31

Buffing wheel: 31

C

Cable, armored: clamping, 75; inspecting, 73

Caulking: applying to siding, 101; holster for caulking gun, 101; irons, 86

Chimney: cleaning, 68, 70; inspecting, 11, 68; installing rain cap, 68, 71; repairing crown, 68, 70

Circuit breakers: match to wire gauge, 20, 73

Contracting: 26

Cracks, ceiling and wall: in basement, 15, 16; in foundation, 122; patching corners, 99; patching curves, 99; patching with fiberglass and acrylic, 97-98; patching with fiberglass and joint compound, 98; patching with mortar, 123; signs of structural problems, 16, 18

D

Doors: and signs of structural problems, 18

Doors, repairing hinged: 58; aligning strike plate, 61; and moisture, 58; planing edges, 62; raising door, 61; reinforcing weak joints, 63; shimming hinges, 58, 61; squaring panel door, 62; tightening hinges, 58

Doors, repairing pocket: 58, 63; adjusting top rollers, 65; and

moisture, 58; pulling jammed door, 64; removing door from frame, 64; replacing rollers, 65; shaving binding stud, 64

Downspouts: inspecting, 10, 11

Drip edge: installing, 94

Driveways, inspecting: 10

E

Efflorescence: 15

Electrical system: matching capacity to load, 73; materials and tools for, 73; and plumbing for ground, 82. *See also* Amperage; Receptacles; Service panel; Switches; Wiring

Electric meters: appearance and amperage, 21

Exteriors, inspecting: chimney, 11; downspouts, 10, 11; driveways, 10; garage, 10; gutters, 10, 11; insect damage, 10, 14; retaining walls, 10; roof, 11, 12; surface drainage, 10, 122; walkways, 10; walls, 10, 11, 13-14; water damage, 10

F

Finishes, wood: types and characteristics, 42

Fireplaces: adding rain cap, 71; anatomy, 68; cleaning chimney flue, 68, 70; draft, 68; flue liner, 68; flue test, 69; installing glass screen, 71-72; materials and tools to maintain, 68; repairing chimney crown, 70

Fireplaces, inspecting: 18, 19, 68; for coal and gas, 19

Fire wall: 15

Flashing: inspecting, 11, 90; repairing, 90; resetting, 92

Flooding: evidence of, 15

Floors: inspecting wood, 19; materials and tools for repairing, 52; quieting creaks in, 52; repairing holes and cracks, 52, 53; repairing sags, 52, 53; replacing floor boards, 52; replacing parquet strips, 54; replacing tongue-and-groove boards, 55-56; sanding, 52, 57; signs of heavy sanding, 19; signs of structural problems, 19

Floors, correcting sags: 52, 53, 112; bracing joists, 113, 118-119; materials and tools for, 112; raising floor from inside, 112, 114-115; raising floor from outside, 112, 115-116; repairing studs, 112, 120-121; sill replacement, 112, 116-118; supporting girders, 112, 113

Flue: cleaning, 68, 70; inspecting, 68; liner, 68; testing, 69

Forced-air system: adjusting dampers, 80; flow check, 24

Foundations, repairing: 122; brick, 123-124; cracks, 122, 123; and drainage, 122; materials and tools for, 122; new footings, 124-125

Framework: types, 8, 9

Framing, inspecting: 16

Fuses: adapters for, 74; match to wire gauge, 20, 73, 74; tamperproof, 74

G

Garage, inspecting: 10

Gas-fired furnace: 25

Girt: 8

Ground-fault circuit interrupter (GFCI): uses, 21

Grozing: 38

Gutters: aligning, 90, 95; cleaning, 90; inspecting, 10, 11, 90; patching, 90, 95; patching with fiberglass and acrylic, 99

H

Heater, auxiliary electric: 77; installing, 80-81

Heat gun: used to strip paint, 40, 41, 43

Heating systems: inspecting, 24; materials and tools for maintaining, 77. *See also* Gas-fired furnace; Hot-air heating system; Hot-water heating system; Oil burner; Steam heating system

Hot-air heating system: adjusting dampers, 77, 80; checking air flow, 24

Hot-water heating system: bleeding radiators, 77; draining system, 77; repairing leaky valves, 77, 79; servicing expansion tank, 77, 79-80

I

Insect infestation: inspection for, 10, 14

Insulation, inspecting: 17

Interiors, inspecting: cracks in ceilings and walls, 18; fireplaces, 18, 19; floors, 19; kitchen, 18; windows, 19

J

Jacks: 112, 113

K

Kitchens, inspecting: 18

Knobs, porcelain: 30; materials and tools for, 30; restoring, 30

L

Lead: handling paint, 10; for leaded glass, 34; testing water for, 22

Lead knife: 36

Lead wool: 86

Leaks: attic, 15; plumbing, 22

Locks, repairing: 30; bent bolts, 31; materials and tools for, 30; rim type, 31

Locks, rim: anatomy, 31

M

Marble: cleaning, 35; identifying genuine, 34

Marble, repairing: 34; materials and tools for, 34; patching with epoxy, 35

Metal roofing: 12; coating, 91

Mortar: matching color, 111

O

Oil burner: inspecting, 24

Oil finish: 42

Overhang: repairing, 106, 108-109

P

Paint, lead: 10

Paint, removing from iron: 32

Paint, removing from wood: 40; with chemicals, 42; with heat, 43; partial stripping, 40; scraping, 42, 43; from siding,

100; strippers, 40, 41, 42
Pin punch: 45
Pipe, cast-iron drain: 22, 82; patching leaks, 85; replacing a section, 87; resealing joint, 85-86
Pipe, copper: 22; splicing into steel line, 82-84
Pipe, lead: 22, 82
Pipe, plastic: cementing CPVC adapters, 84; splicing into steel line, 82, 83-84
Pipe, steel: 22, 82; adapters for adding plastic and copper sections, 83; inspecting, 22; patching supply line, 82; replacing section, 83-84
Plaster: cracks in, 18
Plaster, repairing: bowed plaster, 46; casting molding, 46, 49; cracks and holes, 46; materials and tools for, 46; patching damaged molding, 46, 48; patching with wallboard, 47-48; shaping molding with template, 46, 50
Plaster washers: 46
Plate, sole and top: 9
Plumbing: caulking, 23; CPVC adapters, 83; dielectric union, 83; and electrical ground, 20, 82; exposed pipes, 22; inspecting, 22-23; leak checks, 22; materials and tools for repairing, 82; shutoff valves, 22; toilets, 23; water heater, 23; water pressure, 23. See also Pipe, cast-iron drain; Pipe, copper; Pipe, plastic; Pipe steel
Professions, building: types and contracting with, 26-27

 R

Radiators: 77-80
Railings, iron, repairing: 30; bolting railing cap, 32-33; materials and tools for, 30; resetting posts, 33; rust removal, 32; stripping paint, 32
Receptacle analyzer: 21
Receptacles: evaluating, 21, 73; and ground-fault circuit interrupters, 21; installing three-slot, 75
Repairs: relationship of exterior

to interior, 18
Retaining walls, inspecting: 10
Roof bracket: 69
Roofs: coating metal, 91; installing drip edge, 94; materials and tools for repairing, 90; mending asphalt shingle, 91; patching slate and wood shingle, 91; reinforcing, 90, 96; repairing, 90; replacing slate, 92, 93; replacing tile, 92, 93; replacing wood shingle, 92, 94; safety on, 69. See also Flashing; Gutters
Roofs, inspecting: 11, 12, 17

 S

Safety: with acrylic compound, 97; with asbestos, 10; in attic, 15; burning paint off, 30, 32; with chemicals, 30, 40; chipping caulk, 100; doing electrical work, 73; with floor sander, 52; with gas-fired furnace, 25; hammering and sawing, 106; handling stucco, 104; with heat gun, 40; inspecting fireplaces, 18; iron-working, 30; with lead paint, 10; with masonry, 30, 106; with paint supplies, 40; with plaster, 46; with plastic pipe, 82; repairing doors and windows, 58; on roofs, 69, 90; sanding, 40; soldering pipes, 82; with stained glass, 34, 37, 39; with steam boilers, 24; working on fireplaces, 68
Sanders: drum, 57; edge, 57; flap, 44; orbital, 44
Sanding: different shapes of moldings, 44; dust, 57; floors, 52, 57; tools for, 44; wood filler, 45
Scrapers, paint: 42, 43
Septic system, evaluating: 22
Service panel, evaluating: 20
Shakes, cedar: 12; replacing, 92, 94
Shellac: as finish, 42; removing, 41
Shingles, asphalt: 12; mending, 91
Shingles, wood: 12; mending, 92, 94
Shrink tubing: 76

Siding, wood: inspecting, 13; replacing boards, 106, 109; signs of structural problems, 13
Slate: 12; replacing, 92, 93
Slate ripper: 92
Soldering: came, 38; copper pipe, 82, 84
Stained glass, repairing: 34, 36-39; bracing bulges, 34, 39; materials and tools for, 34; replacing glass pieces, 34, 36-38; tightening channels, 34, 36
Stains: cleaning marble, 35
Stains (coatings): used on stripped wood, 41
Steam heating system: inspecting, 24; leaky valves, 77; quieting, 78; repairing leaky valve, 77; replacing air vent, 77
Strippers, paint: types and characteristics, 41; use, 40, 42
Stucco: creating texture, 105; patching, 104-105; tools for patching, 104
Stucco walls: indications of structural problems, 14; inspecting, 14
Studs: repairing rotted, 120-121
Sump: 122
Switches: evaluating, 73; replacing, 76

 T

Termites: indication of, 14; shields, 14
Toilet, inspecting: 23
Tongue-and-groove boards: replacing, 55-56
Trim, wood. See Wood trim

 V

Varnish: as finish, 40; removing, 41
Voltage tester: 73

 W

Walkways, inspecting: 10
Walls. See Cracks, ceiling and wall; Exteriors, inspecting; Fire wall; Foundations, repairing; Interiors, inspecting; Retaining

walls; Stucco; Stucco walls
Walls, brick: cleaning, 100, 102-103; indications of mortar failure, 13; inspecting, 13; paint removal, 103; replacing brick, 106, 110-111, 123-124; repointing, 100, 123; sealing, 103
Walls, exterior, repairing: 106; brick, 106; materials and tools for, 106; overhang, 108-109; siding, 109; sills, 107-108
Walls, exterior, weatherproofing: materials and tools for, 100; preparation of wood siding, 100-102; waterproofing masonry, 100, 102-103
Water heater, inspecting: 23
Wells: evaluating water and storage tank, 22
Windows: inspecting, 19; signs of structural problems, 19
Windows, leaded. See Stained glass, repairing
Windows, repairing double-hung: adjusting sash cords, 60; freeing stuck sash, 58; loosening sash channel, 59; materials and tools for, 58, 106; and moisture, 58; patching sills, 106, 107-108; reinforcing sash joint, 60; replacing sash cords, 58, 59-60
Wire gauge: 74
Wiring: armored cable, 73; clamping armored cable, 75; for electric heater, 77, 81; inspecting, 20, 21, 73; knob-and-tube, 21, 73; match to rating of breakers or fuses, 20, 73, 74; replacing insulation, 76; replacing receptacle, 75; replacing switch, 76; routing new cable, 81
Wood fillers: 45; for floor cracks, 53
Wood trim: applying wood filler, 45; cleaners, 41; cleaning, 40; finishes for, 42; materials and tools for refinishing, 40; preparing for finish, 40; removing fragile, 40, 44-45; renewing finish, 40; sanding, 44; scraping paint, 42, 43; stains for, 41; stripping with chemicals, 40, 42-43; stripping with heat, 40
Wythe: 9

Time-Life Books is a division of Time Life Inc.

PRESIDENT and CEO: John M. Fahey Jr.

TIME-LIFE BOOKS

MANAGING EDITOR: Roberta Conlan

Director of Design: Michael Hentges
Editorial Production Manager:
  Ellen Robling
Senior Editors: Russell B. Adams Jr.,
  Janet Cave, Lee Hassig, Robert
  Somerville, Henry Woodhead
Director of Operations: Eileen Bradley
Director of Photography and Research:
  John Conrad Weiser
Library: Louise D. Forstall

PRESIDENT: John D. Hall

*Vice President, Director of New Product
  Development:* Neil Kagan
*Associate Director, New Product
  Development:* Quentin S. McAndrew
Marketing Director: James Gillespie
Vice President, Book Production: Marjann
  Caldwell
Production Manager: Marlene Zack
Quality Assurance Manager: James King

HOME REPAIR AND IMPROVEMENT

SERIES EDITOR: Lee Hassig
Administrative Editor: Barbara Levitt

Editorial Staff for *The Old House*
Art Director: David Neal Wiseman
Picture Editor: Catherine Chase Tyson
Text Editor: Esther Ferington
Associate Editors/Research-Writing:
  Annette Scarpitta, Karen Sweet
Technical Art Assistant: Angela Miner
Copyeditor: Judith Klein
Picture Coordinator: Paige Henke
Editorial Assistant: Amy S. Crutchfield

Special Contributors: John Drummond
  (illustration); Jennifer Gearhart, Marvin
  Shultz, Eileen Wentland (digital illustration);George Constable (text); Mel
  Ingber (index).

Correspondents: Christine Hinze (London),
  Christina Lieberman (New York), Maria
  Vincenza Aloisi (Paris).

PICTURE CREDITS

Cover: Photograph, Michael Latil. Art,
  Peter J. Malamas/Totally Incorporated.

Illustrators: Jack Arthur, Terry Atkinson,
  Frederic F. Bigio from B-C Graphics,
  Roger C. Essley, Forte, Inc., William J.
  Hennessy Jr., Elsie Hennig, Walter
  Hilmers Jr., Fred Holz, Dick Lee, John
  Martinez, John Massey, Peter McGinn,
  Joan McGurren, Bill McWilliams, Eduino
  Pereira, Ray Skibinski, Snowden Associ-
  ates, Inc., Whitman Studio, Inc.

Photographers: (Credits from left to right
  are separated by semicolons; from top
  to bottom by dashes.) **End papers:**
  Renée Comet. **10:** Georgia-Pacific;
  Tycomm; Southern Pine Council (2)—
  Terry A. Smiley; Alan Klehr; BHP Steel
  Products USA, Inc.; Tycomm. **21:** Nancy
  Hutchinson (3). **25, 31, 36, 43, 45, 46,
  48, 69, 73, 86, 92, 94, 98:** Renée
  Comet.

ACKNOWLEDGMENTS

Bryon Blose, Long's Corporation, Fairfax,
Va.; Greg Cumming, Accurate Air, Inc.,
Fairfax, Va.; Theresa Dagenhart, Long's
Corporation, Fairfax, Va.; Divine Brothers
Company, Engineering Department, Utica,
N.Y.; Ashley Eldridge, National Chimney
Sweep Guild, Ashland, Va.; Larry Golds-
berry, Behr Process Corporation, Santa
Ana, Calif.; Steve Hancook, Landis & Gyr
Energy Management, Lafayette, Ind.; Ellen
Kardell, Kardell Studio, Washington, D.C.;
Everett Long, Long's Corporation, Fairfax,
Va.; Bob Lyons, William Zinsser and
Company, Somerset, N.J.; Mike McLintock,
Elk Corporation, Dallas; Robert Neveu,
Mestek, Inc. (Space Pak System), West-
field, Mass.; Joe Teets, Fairfax, Va.; Richard
Valentine, Simpson Cleaning Systems,
Clearwater, Fla.; Dan Worley, The Roof
Center, Alexandria, Va.

**Library of Congress
Cataloging-in-Publication Data**
The old house / by the editors of Time-Life
  Books.
  p. cm. — (Home repair and improve-
    ment)
Includes index.
ISBN 0-7835-3898-7
1. Dwellings—Maintenance and repair—
  Amateurs' manuals. 2. Dwellings—
  Remodeling—Amateurs' manuals.
I. Time-Life Books. II. Series.
TH4817.3.O43 1995
643'.7—dc20   95-39668